THEOLOGY IN THE CONTEXT
OF SCIENCE

THEOLOGY IN THE CONTEXT OF SCIENCE

John Polkinghorne

First published in Great Britain in 2008

Society for Promoting Christian Knowledge
36 Causton Street
London SW1P 4ST

British Library Cataloguing-in-Publication Data
A catalogue record for this book is available from the British Library

ISBN 978–0–281–05916–4

1 3 5 7 9 10 8 6 4 2

Typeset by Graphicraft Ltd, Hong Kong
Printed in Great Britain by Ashford Colour Press

Produced on paper from sustainable forests

To the memory of the late Arthur Peacocke

Contents

Preface		ix
Introduction		xi
1	Contextual theology	1
2	Discourse	13
3	Time and space	33
4	Persons and value	46
5	Consonance: creation, providence, and relationality	66
6	Motivated belief	84
7	Eschatology	102
Postscript: Understanding		110
Notes		113
Index		119

Preface

————◆◆————

Much of the material of this book was incorporated into the John Henry Hall lectures at the University of Victoria, British Columbia, which I was privileged to give in October 2008. I am very grateful for the invitation to give the lectures and for the generous hospitality I received while doing so.

I wish to dedicate this book to the memory of my friend and colleague, the late Revd Dr Arthur Peacocke. Arthur made many important contributions to the contemporary dialogue between science and theology and he was the founding Warden of the Society of Ordained Scientists. All of us with a concern to take seriously those two great human endeavours to explore reality, science, and religion, are permanently in his debt.

John Polkinghorne
Queens' College, Cambridge

Introduction

————◆◆◆————

The past fifty years have seen the growth and flourishing of what have come to be called contextual theologies. The particular experiences and challenges that arise in a specific setting – whether its character is social and cultural (feminist insights; the liberation insights of the poor; and so on), or geographical and cultural (South-East Asia; Africa; and so on) – came to be recognised as providing new and stimulating ways of shaping theological thought. Of course, any particular viewpoint offers not only the prospect of new lines of sight, but it also carries with it the threat of new tricks of perspective. Yet these contextual developments have largely been welcomed, and their reception by the theological community has been positive.

This is in contrast to the way in which most theologians have related to the insights coming from another cultural context of considerable contemporary influence, namely that of modern science. The past fifty years also saw the growth and flourishing of much activity in the area of science and religion, but the manner in which this has been reported and received in the theological community at large has been different from the way in which that community has responded to insights derived from other specific contexts. There has certainly been a degree of awareness among theologians that a vigorous discussion is going on in the world of science and theology, but the books written, and the resources thus offered, have largely been conceived in the specific style of an ancillary, problem-tackling activity, concerned with a number of discrete and somewhat specialised issues (creation and cosmology; divine action and the laws of nature; and so on), rather than offering also a source of more general insight, expressed through shaping a style of theological thinking. I must confess that much of my own writing has been in the problem-oriented mode.

Because of the narrowness of the approach that has actually been taken in the interaction with science, it seems likely that a potentially helpful theological resource has been neglected. Of course, I am not suggesting that science can answer theology's questions for it, but simply proposing that there is a strategy for seeking truth through motivated belief which is natural in the context of science and which should be capable of useful extension beyond the latter's domain of proper concern, to yield also a particular way of framing theological discourse.

The style of thought naturally associated with the context of science has the character of what I have called 'bottom-up thinking'.[1] It seeks to evaluate the evidential particularities of experience before attempting to move to the formulation of wider forms of understanding. Scientists are wary of general arguments that fail to be submitted to the discipline of being sifted and assessed by comparison with specific instances. Often it is only the stubborn character of the reality actually encountered that is able to mould adequately the shape of our thought. Quite frequently it is found that modes of thinking are required which are counterintuitive in terms of prior rational expectation. The paradigm example from physics is the idiosyncratic nature of the subatomic quantum world.

If theological discussion is to proceed in the context of science in the way suggested, its account of divine creation must take fully into consideration the actual nature of the universe that we observe and the character of its history, both in its apparent fruitfulness and in its apparent wastefulness. Theology should not rest content with simply an abstract discussion of the concept of creation out of nothing. To take another example, the kind of logical and grammatical discussions concerning the meaning of the simplicity of the divine nature, or concerning the kind of atemporality that properly belongs to God – issues that so greatly occupied the thought of people in the later Middle Ages and that are the prime concern of many philosophical theologians today – have to be supplemented by more particular considerations. Close attention must be given of the actual detail of the data of divine revelatory disclosure and the way in which this constrains and sharpens the conclusions of general argument. Theology's concern is with the God of Abraham, Isaac, and Jacob as well as with the God of the philosophers. (Of course, it has also to take account of what other world faiths have to say about the nature of divinity.) To do so is not to devalue philosophical analysis, but to suggest that its attempted generality must be held in tension with the particularities of creation and revelation. Theodicy is high on the agenda of theology pursued in the context of science, as is a serious engagement with the significance of temporality, not only for creatures but also for the Creator (see chapter 3). The common academic convention of maintaining a degree of separation between systematic theology and biblical studies seems strange to the scientist, rather as if theory and experiment were to be assigned to different departments within physics, rather than inextricably intertwining with each other. Of course, individual scholars have their particular specialisations, but these should be pursued in active dialogue with colleagues with collateral interests.

I believe, therefore, that the field of science and religion should be treated as another form of contextual theology, rather than its role being seen simply as that of providing useful information which can be referred to as seems necessary – usually rather briefly and often as part of an apologetic exercise. The dialogue between science and religion can rightly seek to contribute to creative theological thinking itself, in complementary relationship with other forms of contextual theology. Failure on the part of most mainstream theologians to take this attitude provides, I believe, an explanation of a feeling among participants in the science and religion community that their work is often not taken with sufficient seriousness by many of their systematic theological colleagues. Most scientist-theologians are somewhat reticent about expressing this feeling, but I believe it to be quite widespread, and I think that it is intellectually healthy to acknowledge that this is so. I do not think that this unease is simply an indication of folie de grandeur on the part of our community. We know that what we have to offer is limited, and that by itself it is certainly insufficient for the great task of theological exploration, but our work deserves more than the occasional footnote.

This book is intended as a concise attempt to see what a scientific contextual theology might look like. According to what has been said, the project is presented as one that seeks to offer a distinctive style of thought and argument, as well as serving to provide a specific source of response to particular issues. This includes a rebuttal of the scientistic claim, so often asserted today, of total scientific relevance and total theological irrelevance in the academy, a judgement which from time to time comes thundering across from the more polemical members of the atheistic community. What is being attempted in this volume stands in a kind of complementary relationship to an earlier book of mine, *Science and the Trinity*,[2] which sought to redress another form of imbalance by allowing theology to set a greater part of the agenda for the interdisciplinary dialogue between science and religion. My present concern focuses principally on the character of that dialogue, though of course specific issues will also arise in the course of the discussion. A number of the specific ideas discussed in this book can be found treated in detail elsewhere in the rapidly expanding literature dealing with science and religion, including discussions in my own writing. However, the way in which the material is here organised and presented differs from much of the latter form of writing, in a manner that corresponds to the difference between seeking general insight on the one hand and solving specific problems on the other. I hope that the resulting tone of discourse will result in a book that will be found interesting and accessible by a wide range of readers. Yet I must confess that in writing it I have also had in mind a particular audience, made up of theological students either at university or elswhere (and even, one might hope, practising theologians), some of whom I would like to try to entice into taking into account with an enhanced degree of interest what the context of science can offer to theology as a whole. With this target in mind, as well as the needs of the general reader, I have not sought to go into more scientific detail than has seemed necessary in order to indicate the potential insight that I believe is made available by the pursuit of theology in the context of science. What is offered here is a programmatic indication of the value of the scientific contextual approach, rather than an exhaustive account of all matters that could be considered relevant.

Chapter 1 emphasises that theology has always been done in some particular context. Inevitably, what is offered is a view from somewhere. Examples drawn from the interactions with science, attempted by the small number of contemporary theologians concerned with such issues, suggest that the failure to make full use of the potentiality inherent in the scientific context has often arisen from conceptual confusions which could have been dispelled by closer attention to what the scientist-theologians – writers with a professional knowledge of science and a serious interest in theology – have actually had to say.

I am claiming that a substantial part of the influence of a contextual theology arises from the particular style of discourse in which it is naturally expressed. Of course, as I have already acknowledged, that gift in itself can be ambiguous, with the possibility of imposing narrowness of vision instead of offering breadth of understanding. The rise of deism, and eventually atheism, in the eighteenth century was undoubtedly due partly to the encouragement that contemporary science then appeared to give to a mechanistic mode of thought. However, in the twentieth century, science's picture of the physical world was drastically revised in the light of the discoveries of quantum theory and relativity. The clear and determinate world of Newtonian physics was replaced by something altogether more strange and subtle. The idea of mere mechanism simply died.

Chapter 2 discusses the changed manner of scientific discourse that has resulted from these twentieth-century scientific developments, and the implications of this for theology conducted in the context of science. Commonsense thinking is no longer to be considered an adequate guide to the character of physical process, and the more subtle approach that has proved necessary in science bears a degree of cousinly relationship to theology's wrestling with the mystery of deity.

The loss of what had previously seemed to be an unproblematic objectivity led physicists to appeal to intelligibility as the proper ground for belief in the reality of the physical world, including the existence of intrinsically unseen realities such as quarks. Modern physics also makes it plain that quantum entities can only be known in a manner that is in accord with their Heisenbergian uncertainty, thereby pointing to the fact that there is no universal form that epistemology has to take. The forms of knowledge appropriate to the everyday world and to the quantum world have completely different characters.

These insights are helpful to theology's thinking in its own domain, and a kinship may be discerned between these two great forms of truth-seeking discourse.[3] The unexpected strangeness and counterintuitive character of the physical world means that the instinctive question for a scientist to ask is not, 'Is it reasonable?', as if one knew beforehand the shape that rationality had to take, but the question, 'What makes you think that might be the case?', an enquiry open to the unexpected but demanding evidence to support the actual answer given. This readiness to accept well-motivated belief, however surprising its character might turn out to be, should encourage theology to adopt the bottom-up approach of grounding its own beliefs in actual experience, including the record of revelatory events in which the divine will and nature are believed to have been most clearly manifested. The interpretation of these disclosure events will necessarily involve subtle acts of evaluation, since revelation does not take the form of propositions unproblematically presented for unquestionable acceptance. Rather, revelation is the indispensable record of foundationally significant human encounters with sacred reality. The essence of rationality is the conformation of our mode of thought to the nature of the reality that we are seeking to think about. Just as there is no universal epistemology, so there is no universal form that rationality has to take. Once again, the difference between classical thinking and quantum thinking makes the point clearly enough in a scientific context. In the former case one has classical logic, with its law of the excluded middle (there is no intermediate possibility between 'A' or 'not-A'), but in the latter case a different (quantum) logic is found to hold[4] (since quantum theory can mix together seemingly incompatible possibilities, such as 'here' and 'there').

In both science and theology, the intertwining of experience and interpretation implies a degree of circularity, but this need not invalidate rational commitment to well-winnowed and well-motivated beliefs. In both disciplines, inference to the best explanation is a legitimate strategy to pursue. Neither science nor religion has access to absolute truth, indubitable beyond the possibility of a challenge. The kinship thus discerned between science and theology in their respective fields of search for truthful understanding rebuts the strident claims made by some atheists that theology is not a proper subject with a rightful place in the academy.

A different kind of discourse arises from the fact that an important element in many contextual theologies is provided by the ethical insights and demands that they articulate, as when liberation theology speaks of an option for the poor. Pure science is concerned simply with the search for truthful knowledge, but its offspring technology then takes that knowledge and uses it to acquire the power to get things done that were not possible previously. Yet not everything that can be done should be done and, if right choices are to be made, wisdom must be added to the gifts of knowledge and power. Science's formal distancing of itself from issues of value, expressed in the way in which it frames its argument in terms of what is found to happen rather than what ought to happen, means that scientists must look beyond their discipline for help in addressing ethical issues. Chapter 2 concludes by briefly considering some of the general implications of what is involved in this ethical quest.

The temporal and spatial character of human experience is fundamental to the thought of both science and theology. Science's discovery of the significance of evolutionary processes at work over vast spans of history means that the role of time is not merely that of a means of indexing when events happened, but it has a formative role in bringing about the character of the present. What is now has to be understood in the light of what has been. For theology this means that a concept of continuously developing creation must play an essential part in its thinking.

Both science and theology face perplexities in relation to their understanding of the true nature of time. Chapter 3 considers these issues. While science constrains what can be said about such matters, it is not of itself sufficient to determine unique answers. Ultimately metaphysical decisions are required, which have to be made and defended on metaphysical grounds. It is perfectly proper for theological considerations to play a part in this process. The point is well illustrated by a discussion of the flow of time. Does our impression of the passage of time correspond to the fact that we actually live in a universe of unfolding becoming, or is that feeling simply a trick of human psychological perspective, imposed on us in a block universe whose true nature is held to correspond to the atemporal reality of the entire space-time continuum? The latter concept has a degree of affinity with classical theology's picture of God's relationship to a creation seen from eternity 'all at once'; the former concept has an affinity with modern open theology. An evolving creation, in which the character of the present is constituted by the specificity of the past, suggests the theological possibility of a true divine engagement with created temporality. This view leads to the idea of a dipolarity of eternity/temporality in the divine nature, embraced as a free kenotic decision on the part of a Creator who has chosen to relate in a temporal manner to the historically unfolding story of creation. This development provides a good illustration of how taking the context of science seriously can encourage a particular way of enhancing the conceptual scope of theological thinking. The openness of the resulting metaphysical picture can also be held to suggest a kenosis of divine omniscience, in which even God does not yet know the unformed future.

The concept of personhood is one of central concern for theology. At first sight it might seem that this is a topic on which the context of science might exercise little influence, since scientific investigation concerns itself solely with the impersonal dimensions of reality. Even neuroscience is not in a position to offer very much help. Its current investigations into brain processes, interesting and important though they are, still confront an unbridged gulf between the discourse of neural processing and the simplest forms of personal mental experience, such as seeing red or feeling hungry. The 'hard problems' of consciousness are hard indeed.

Much of science's great success has come from the secret weapon of experiment, a means of gaining knowledge which is conferred on it precisely by science's self-defining concentration on impersonal reality, thus permitting the repetition of particular investigations as often as desired. Yet chapter 4 points out that much more needs to be said about the actual practice of science itself than can be articulated in the formally impersonal discourse that science has chosen to adopt.

The fact is that if we are truly to understand what is happening in the world, a great enlargement of conceptual scope is required, taking the enquirer beyond the narrow limits imposed by scientific protocol. The deep intelligibility of the universe – a remarkable fact that science is happy enough to exploit but unable to explain – is nevertheless so significant a feature of the world as surely to demand its being treated as more than a happy accident. Beneath the surface appearance of the physical universe there lies a fundamental realm of profound order and rational beauty. One could say that science has discovered that the fabric of the cosmos is shot through with signs of mind, but it does not know why this should be so. Theology can render this discovery intelligible, through its understanding that the Mind of the Creator is the source of the wonderful order of the world.

The role of tacit skills of judgement exercised in scientific research, so insightfully explored by Michael Polanyi,[5] makes it clear that the practice of a formally impersonal science is nevertheless intrinsically an activity of persons, having a character that means that it could never be delegated to a well-programmed computer. In its turn, theology in the context of science has to take the psychosomatic nature of human beings very seriously. Some modest help is afforded here by an enlargement taking place in science's own set of conceptual resources, due to contemporary developments in the study of complex systems. These have suggested the necessity of complementing the traditional reductionist story of physics, framed in terms of exchanges of energy between constituents, with an holistic account employing a developed concept of 'active information'. This work is at a very preliminary stage, but it promises to afford an enriched scientific context which should be of real value to theology.

Other topics considered in chapter 4 include the need for an adequate understanding of the full context of evolutionary process, the nature of consciousness, and the role of value. The latter topic, together with that of the deep cosmic intelligibility already noted, offers the possibility of a revised approach to natural theology, understood as being in a complementary relationship to science, rather than as an attempt to rival it in its proper domain, and concerned with understanding what science itself has to treat merely as brute fact. The claimed achievement of this new natural theology is satisfying insight rather than indubitable proof. Scientific questions may indeed be expected to receive scientific answers, but there are many questions which are both meaningful and necessary to ask, but which lie outside the self-limited confines of science. Some of these are metaquestions that arise from the experience of doing science, but which then take the enquirer beyond its narrow borders.

Chapter 5 turns from the rather general ways in which the context of science can influence styles of theological discourse, in order to consider three specifically focused points of contact: creation, providence, and relationality. Involved in each case is a topic (the history of the universe, the causal character of cosmic process, the remarkable degree of interconnectedness present in the physical world) about whose understanding both science and theology have things to say. Of course, their perspectives are distinct and the questions that they address are different. There is no logical entailment from one discipline to the other, but one may rightly expect to be able to discern a degree of consonance between what each has to say.

The doctrine of creation asserts the sustaining will of God to be the ground of continuing cosmic history. Science's discovery of the rational transparency and rational beauty of the physical world is certainly consonant with the understanding that the structure of the universe is shaped by the Mind of its Creator. The remarkable set of scientific insights assembled under the rubric of the Anthropic Principle has shown that a universe capable of developing carbon-based life is a very particular world indeed, having had to be endowed with a very specific physical fabric in order to permit this fruitful possibility. This unanticipated scientific discovery is certainly congruent with belief that cosmic history is an expression of the fruitful purposes of the universe's Creator. The evolutionary character of the universe is consonant with a theological understanding that God's act of creation is a kenotic act of divine self-limitation, bringing into being a world in which creatures are allowed 'to make themselves'. In a creation of this kind, death is the necessary cost of the development of new life, and physical process has to operate 'at the edge of chaos', in regimes where chance and necessity, order and disorder, interlace. These scientific insights offer theology some modest help as it seeks to wrestle with the perplexing questions of theodicy. There is an inescapable shadow side to the fertility of evolutionary process.

Science's account of physical process is patchy (for example it is not fully understood how quantum physics and classical physics relate to each other) and it is characterised by widespread intrinsic unpredictabilities (as in quantum theory and chaos theory). Moreover, the nature of causality is not an issue capable of being settled by science alone, for it requires also an act of metaphysical decision. It is certainly clear that science has not established the causal closure of the world on its own naturalistic terms. In fact, it is perfectly possible to take the actually substantiated conclusions of physics and incorporate them into a metaphysical scheme that is compatible with the exercise of agency, both by human persons and by divine providence. The picture of a God whose interaction with creation operates within the open grain of nature has implications for theological expectations about the character of prayer and the discernment of providence.

In the twentieth century, science discovered remarkable degrees of relationality present in the physical world, at all levels from the subatomic to the cosmological. Understanding our apparent everyday experience of the separability of objects is far from being an unproblematically straightforward matter. This picture of a deeply relational universe is consonant with a theological belief in the trinitarian nature of that world's Creator.

This chapter illustrates how scientific insight can suggestively illuminate theological discourse, without pretending to determine it. The exploration of a complementary consonance between science and theology is the reason why there is no single chapter in the book with the heading 'God'. Rather than a self-contained analysis of the kind associated in works of philosophical theology with the topic De Deo Uno, the intertwining of scientific and theological insights, so natural to the discourse of this book, encourages treating the topic of deity in via, so to speak, as the manifold aspects of the divine economy, manifested in the works of creation, pass under review.

Scientists are often suspicious of religious belief because they think that it is based on unquestioning submission to an unchallengeable authority. I believe this to be a disastrous mistake on their part. Chapter 6 seeks to indicate how one may present motivations for Christian belief, using a bottom-up style of reasoning that moves from evidence to understanding in just the manner that we have seen to be appropriate to argument presented in the context of science. It is important that theology does not lose its nerve about appealing to the unique significance of revelatory events. As a test case, the discussion of the chapter centres on the resurrection of Jesus Christ, first considering the coherence of the idea of miracle and then indicating reasons for taking seriously the New Testament evidential claims of the appearances of the risen Christ and the finding of the empty tomb. The chapter concludes by moving outside the Christian context to acknowledge and discuss the perplexing issue of the apparent cognitive clashes that exist between the beliefs of the different world faith traditions.

Science's naturalistic stories always end in the eventual futility of death, not only in the case of individuals, but even in the case of the universe itself. Theology is able to speak of the hope of a destiny beyond death because it can appeal beyond current transience to the everlasting faithfulness of God. Science cannot speak about that kind of hope – either for it or against it – but its context does have some influence on how one might try to think about the credibility of the idea of a life beyond death for human beings. This contextual influence arises because a coherent idea of the possibility of the continuance of individual life post mortem requires fulfilling conditions of both continuity and discontinuity, issues that are considered in chapter 7. The condition of continuity must be sufficient to ensure that it really is the same persons who died who are the ones that live again. The traditional carrier of continuity between life in this world and life in the world to come has been the soul. Yet the context of science encourages a psychosomatic view of humanity, which would prohibit the soul from being conceived in dualist terms as a detachable spiritual component, released at death from the fleshly entrapment of the body. However, the increasing recognition of the significance of the concept of information encourages reconceiving the soul as the almost infinite information-bearing pattern carried by the matter of the body, a pattern which it is perfectly coherent to believe will be preserved by God beyond death and re-embodied in an ultimate eschatological act of resurrection. Those thus made alive again are surely not intended simply to die again, so that there is also a condition of discontinuity requiring that the 'matter' of the world to come shall not be subject to the thermodynamic drift to disorder that brings about futility in this world. Discussion indicates that it seems coherent to believe that God can bring about such a new form of matter.

A brief concluding postscript stresses that science and theology share in the great human quest for truth and understanding and that their fruitful interaction derives from this common concern.

1

Contextual theology

All theology is done in a context. The accounts that the theologians give us are not utterances delivered from some point of lofty detachment, independent of culture – views from nowhere, as it were – but they are all views from somewhere, offering finite and particular human perspectives onto the infinite reality of God. Each such perspective not only offers an opportunity for insight, but it is also open to the danger of imposing limitation and distortion. Specificity of context will make some aspects of the divine will and nature more readily accessible to theological recognition and understanding, while at the same time hiding others from easy view.

The earliest Christian theologians, the authors of the New Testament, wrote in the context of their heritage of contemporary Judaism and in varying degrees of engagement with the surrounding Graeco-Roman culture. Their writings offer unique and irreplaceable access to the story of the life, death, and resurrection of Jesus Christ, together with indispensable accounts of how his first followers experienced and understood the life-transforming power that they believed had come to them from the risen Christ, mediated in the Church by the continuing work of the Holy Spirit. This means that these New Testament writings, together with the Old Testament books of the Hebrew Bible which were the New Testament authors' own scriptural context, create a biblical setting which is of fundamental importance for all subsequent Christian thinking. Yet this acknowledgement of the unique significance of scripture is by no means enough to establish an unambiguous and sufficient context for theology.

The biblical texts, which are often very concise in their expression of deep and challenging truths, stand in need of continuing exploratory interpretation, conducted in each succeeding Christian generation. Within the canon of the New Testament itself one finds

1

a number of different treatments of theological themes, doubtless formulated within the different contexts that corresponded to the various early Christian communities in which oral tradition was propagated and the original documents eventually written. A comparison of the Pauline and Johannine writings, together with consideration of the approach taken by the unknown author of the Epistle to the Hebrews, makes this clear enough. The common affirmation of the unique status of Jesus, crucified and risen, is expressed by the different authors in contrasting ways which serve to complement each other.

The Christian theologian will see scripture as divinely inspired but humanly written. Its authors were inevitably influenced by the cultural context of their times, and a major exegetical task is to discriminate between what in their writings is of lasting significance and what is simply contemporary understanding to which we do not owe an unrevisable allegiance. Science has played a useful part in assisting these acts of judgement, so that, for example, when the psalmist says that God 'has established the world; it shall never be moved' (Psalm 93:1), we are able to recognise that he is using the cosmological understanding of his day to express the Creator's faithfulness, rather than making a statement about the structure of the solar system. Galileo was to argue thus, making a point to which we shall return shortly.

In any case, the hermeneutic quest should not simply be for a single exclusive kind of interpretation, since there are a variety of levels at which the texts may properly be read.[1] Such richness of meaning is a common feature of all profound forms of literature, which always hold out the prospect of an overplus of significance awaiting the open and receptive reader. The notion of a plain text with a single meaning may suit the cookery book, but it will not do for writing that sets out to explore the multiple richness and depth of reality, either human or divine. The history of theological thought provides abundant examples of the recognition of the need for a many-levelled approach to scripture. In the patristic period, many of the Fathers used a scheme that discerned four dimensions of scriptural interpretation, corresponding to literal, symbolic, moral, and spiritual meanings. Even in a period such as Reformation times, when there was a greater tendency to employ a less nuanced interpretative strategy, and people were inclined to accept the idea that there is a plain meaning to be found in the scriptural text that anyone who runs may read, the fact is that this approach actually led to a wide variety of different interpretative conclusions. Such diversity indicates clearly enough how problematic it is to suppose the irrelevance of particular contextual influences in shaping biblical interpretation. There is more than one way to strike a balance between the Epistle of James and the Epistle to the Romans in forming a theological concept of the role of good works.

The polysemic nature of scripture is sometimes a problem for scientists, who are often more used to the sharp clarity of mathematical argument. Yet even in mathematics not all is expressed on the surface. Kurt Gödel showed that axiomatised systems, sufficiently complex to contain the integers, cannot establish their own consistency. If they are assumed to be consistent, then it can be shown that they contain mathematical truths that are expressible, but not provable, within the confines of the system. Thus even here, in this most abstract of subjects, the richness of reality eludes tight specification. Truth is more than theoremhood.

While a few religiously minded scientists have been tempted to treat the Bible as though it were a textbook in which one could look up the ready-made answers to every theological question, a better metaphor is surely that of the laboratory notebook, in which are recorded accounts of foundational encounters involving acts of divine self-disclosure, essential for theological theory-making, but leading to and needing further reflective interpretation. Revelation itself is experiential rather than propositional. It provides the raw material for the work of the bottom-up theological thinker, seeking truth through assessment of the motivations for belief.

At certain times, a particular contemporary philosophical style has moulded the context of thought, substantially influencing the resulting shape of theological discourse, without completely determining its character. Augustine was heavily influenced by the neo-platonism of his day, and Aquinas owed much to the recovery of a lost Aristotelianism that took place in the course of the thirteenth century. Yet neither slavishly followed their philosophical mentors at every point. For example, Aquinas rejected Aristotelian belief in the eternity of the world. In the nineteenth century, and on into the twentieth, many German theologians have seemed to write with Kant looking over one shoulder and Hegel looking over the other. The process philosophy of Alfred North Whitehead has substantially influenced a number of present-day scientist-theologians, most notably Ian Barbour.[2] The power structure of the community within which theology is being pursued has also been a contextual influence. The pre-Constantinian Church, marginalised in society and subjected to bouts of persecution, had a different outlook to that of the post-Constantinian Church, enjoying a comfortable alliance with the state. The resulting transformation of spiritual and theological style induced as a consequent counter-movement the emergence of monasticism. Social sensitivities change, as when Christian people came, after eighteen centuries, at last to recognise that the institution of slavery was incompatible with a true concept of the dignity and worth of every human person.

The advance of general human knowledge has also often influenced theological judgements. In his Literal Commentary on Genesis, Augustine acknowledged that if a traditional interpretation of scripture was found to be untenable in the light of well-established conclusions of secular knowledge, then that interpretation would need to be reconsidered – a dictum to which Galileo was later to make an appeal. In actual fact it has often turned out that matters which had previously been taken for granted by almost all people as being items of common knowledge, such as the fixity of the Earth or the fixity of species, when found scientifically to be in need of revision, were discovered not to be indispensable to theology either. Moreover, it has frequently been the case that Christian thought has been able to benefit from the incorporation of new secular insights. In the nineteenth century, Aubrey Moore, recognising that a theological understanding of evolution implied that God was not a detached and distant Creator, but had chosen to operate through the natural processes by which creatures made themselves, said that Charles Darwin 'under the guise of a foe, did the work of a friend'.[3] This kind of positive interaction should occasion no surprise. Search for knowledge of God is the quest for the most profound and comprehensive form of understanding, a task to which contributions from all truth-seeking enterprises will be both welcome and necessary.

These very general contextual influences have been active in varying degrees in every period of theological thinking. Yet we have noted that the second half of the twentieth century saw a particularly enhanced recognition of explicitly contextual modes of thought, and a resulting extensive deployment of the resources that they provide. The style of this contemporary contextual theology is largely that which Rowan Williams has called 'communicative': making forays into religiously neutral intellectual territory in order to gain new insight through participation in the local culture, while at the same time exploring translations of theological statements into the local dialect.[4] A portfolio of such theological approaches has been developed, explicitly located within specific domains of experience and insight. As a consequence, one may expect surveys of the contemporary theological scene to include chapters with headings such as 'Liberation Theology' (drawing particularly on the experiences and needs of the poor in developing countries), 'Feminist Theology' (based on the distinctive perspectives of women, and often severely critical of what is perceived as still being a male-dominated Church and society), or 'Black Theology' (drawing on the experiences and insights of black people).[5] In addition, such surveys are likely to contain chapters overtly related to theological thinking in specific geographical and cultural regions ('South-East Asian Theology', 'African Theology', and so on). Books of this survey kind will also often have a chapter or two on the relationship between science and theology, but the rubric under which this topic is presented is unlikely to be phrased in contextual terms. I do not think that the title of this book would be a likely chapter heading. This stylistic difference is symptomatic of an underlying unsatisfactoriness in the relationship between science-based understanding and the mainstream of theological enquiry. There has been a tendency to think of theology's relationship with science simply in terms of wrestling with specific issues and problems, such as creation or divine action, rather than in the general terms that would recognise the scientific context as affording also an opportunity to make use of an intellectual style of thinking of a more widely insightful kind. Of course, specific frontier issues will always be significant foci for interaction, and chapter 5 will look at some of these, but the style of discourse appropriate to the science-and-religion perspective is also something to be accepted and valued in itself.

To put the matter bluntly, I believe that too many theologians fail to treat what science has to offer with the appropriate degree of seriousness that would enable them to acknowledge adequately its contextual role. There are various reasons why this might be the case. One, of course, is an understandable anxiety about getting involved with matters concerning which one does not possess technical mastery. No doubt the details of science often seem opaque and impossibly demanding to those outside it. As a scientist-theologian I can readily understand this feeling, since I face similar problems in my forays into theology, in the course of which I am only too aware of lacking the kind of expertise that can only be gained through a lifetime of scholarly study in a single discipline. The traditional vocabulary of trinitarian theology has its own kind of opacity. Yet if interdisciplinary work is to be undertaken at all, we have to be prepared to accept the intellectual risks involved. Without sticking our necks out a little, we shall not be able to see very far. No one can come to the interdisciplinary task with a range of knowledge so complete that all sense of precariousness can be set aside. Yet, such interdisciplinary interaction is essential to the full pursuit of theological enquiry. Since God is the ground of all that is, every kind of human rational investigation of reality must have something to contribute to theological thinking, as the latter pursues its goal of an adequate understanding of the created world, understood in the light of the belief that the mind and purposes of the Creator lie behind cosmic order and history. Every mode of rational exploration of reality will have an offering to make.

As far as interaction with science is concerned, the interdisciplinary task is made more manageable by the fact that it is an engagement with concepts and styles of thought, rather than with highly technical detail, that is required in order to give theologians access to what they really need. Understanding the relevance of general relativity to an adequate account of the nature of created space and time, and its significance in relation to the gravitational properties of matter that have played so important a role in the history of the universe, does not require the theologian to attempt to wrestle with the mathematical intricacies of solutions to Einstein's field equations. There are a number of excellent books for the general educated reader that successfully present scientific concepts in an accessible manner. In addition, there are extensive writings originating in the contemporary science and religion community itself, which offer guides to the exploration of the frontier region between science and theology and provide examples of how people whose intellectual formation has lain in the natural sciences approach questions of religious belief. Yet this substantial body of work is comparatively seldom referred to in any serious way by mainstream theologians. The contrast between this state of affairs and that existing elsewhere between theology and other contextual sources of insight and experience is striking. Theologians know readily enough that they do not need to have lived in a base community in Latin America in order to be able to avail themselves of the insights and critiques of liberation theology. They only need to read with attention the writings of those whose formation has been in that context. Equally, theologians ought to understand that they do not need to have worked in a laboratory, or to be able to read learned scientific journals, in order to be able to avail themselves of the ideas and critiques of the science and religion community. At least some theologians should pay attention to what that community's discourse might have to offer.

One could not deny, however, that some of the responsibility for this neglect lies also with the scientist-theologians themselves. No doubt our amateur writings can lack the depth and sophistication that professional theologians are used to, especially in dealing with such technical subjects as trinitarian theology. No doubt we sometimes display a narrowness of interest. No form of contextual thinking can be free from the limitations intrinsic to its particular perspective. The remedying of such defects has to come from truly interdisciplinary encounter, set up on a wide basis and conducted in a charitable spirit of willingness to learn from the other, not least because of the consciousness of needing one's own view to be enlarged. It is a matter for real regret that, with a few honourable exceptions, mainstream theologians have played only a comparatively minor role in the field of science and religion, seldom participating in conferences or working groups in which the issues have been explored or contributing to the literature.

Another factor that has inhibited interaction between scientists and theologians has been an ideological disinclination to the task on the part of some members of the theological community. In the twentieth century, the tradition stemming from Karl Barth, arguably the most influential theologian of that period, laid such exclusive stress on the primacy of divine self-revelation in Christ as to seem to relegate to insignificance the role of any investigations that looked at the possibility of collateral illumination offered by other sources of insight or ways of seeking truth. The concept of some degree of general revelation, of the kind associated with the exploration of natural theology in a manner like that pursued by Thomas Aquinas in his discussion of faith and reason, was set aside by many theologians. Yet this is just the kind of approach that can prove fruitful in the exchange between science and theology.

However, I have complained enough, and one must also acknowledge that some contemporary theologians have sought to pay attention to what science has to say. One of these is the German Lutheran theologian Wolfhart Pannenberg. He has been emphatic that theology should not confine itself to life in the fideistic ghetto, but it must interact with the whole of human knowledge, including the sciences. Pannenberg has sought a particularly extensive engagement with the human sciences,[6] but he has also made moves that seek to take the natural sciences into account. It is his belief that:

> If the God of the Bible is the creator of the universe, then it is not possible to understand fully or even appropriately the processes of nature without any reference to that God. If, on the contrary, nature can appropriately be understood without reference to the God of the Bible, then God cannot be the creator of the universe, and consequently he cannot be truly God and be trusted as the source of moral teaching either.[7]

Pannenberg clearly declines the Kantian move of accommodating religion to science by assigning the material world to the latter and allocating the moral sphere to religion. My interpretation of his assertion of the indispensability of the biblical God to the enterprise of science is certainly not that theology has the right to prejudge or intervene in the conclusions reached by science in its own legitimate domain. There is good reason to believe that scientifically posable questions should be expected to receive scientifically stateable answers. But not all significant questions lie within science's self-limited power to answer. Once one moves outside the scientific domain, as we shall see one has to do even when considering such issues as the nature of temporality or the nature of causality, theology has a right to contribute to the subsequent metascientific discourse. In addition, there is a further metascientific necessity to make comprehensible the deep intelligibility of the universe, that fundamental fact about the world which has enabled science to derive its explanatory success.[8] This is too remarkable a cosmological feature to be treated as if it were just a brute fact or a happy accident. The scientists' discovery of the remarkable transparency of the universe to rational enquiry can be rendered intelligible by the theologian, who is able to interpret it as the consequence of human encounter with the Mind of that world's Creator, the One who is the true ground of the wonderful order of the universe. Seen in this way, the activity of science is recognised to be an aspect of the imago dei.

Such metascientific questions are certainly important, but they are also very general in their character. Pannenberg has also paid some attention to more specific matters.[9] One of these concerns the role of the concept of inertia in scientific thinking. A physicist understands inertia to be the property of a body's resistance to having its state of motion changed. At the root of the idea lies Newton's first law of motion, asserting the persistence of uniform motion in a straight line in the absence of an impressed force to effect a change. Pannenberg believes that this purely scientific idea induced the metascientific notion that matter possesses an intrinsic ontological persistence, and that therefore it stands in no need of a creator God to sustain it in being. As a matter of historical fact, the growth of deism and atheism in post-Newtonian Europe may well have owed something to this interpretation, and to the contemporary mechanical philosophy that it encouraged. The twentieth-century demise of mere mechanism gives us a salutary reminder that there is nothing absolute or incorrigible about the context of science. It necessarily shares in the provisionality that must to a degree characterise all human knowledge. Recognition of this fact should make us appropriately cautious, but it should not be allowed to induce rational paralysis. At any given time, human beings have to make the best use of the sources of insight that are at their disposal. In relation to any attempted metascientific appeal to inertia, careful reflection makes it clear that science itself can neither affirm material existence as a matter of independent metaphysical necessity, as materialism would assert, nor deny theological belief that inertia is a divinely bestowed and sustained property of created matter. These metascientific issues simply lie outside the limited scope of science to settle. The choice between the metaphysical strategies of materialism and theism has to be made on quite different grounds. Pannenberg's anxieties about the influence of inertial ideas are perfectly reasonable, but the remedy is to be sought in the realm of more careful metaphysical assessment.

Another scientific concept that has been treated as highly significant by Pannenberg is the idea of a field. He frequently invokes it

as a way of speaking of spirit. Here there are real difficulties. A physicist will feel distinctly uneasy when Pannenberg writes 'I rather think
that the modern conceptions of fields and energy went a long way
to "spiritualise" physics'.[10] Many theologians do not seem to understand that Einstein's celebrated equation, $E = mc^2$, can be read both
ways. It as much asserts the materiality of energy as it does the energetic character of matter. Fields are carriers of energy and momentum, just like particles. While global in extent, classical fields are local
in causal structure (changes in different regions can be made that are
independent of each other), and their classical equations are as deterministic as the particle equations of Newtonian mechanics. Quantum
fields are certainly indeterministic and inter-relational, but this is
because of their quantum nature, not their field character. Much more
promising as a possible scientific hint of something akin in nature
to spirit is surely to be found in the concept of 'active information',
beginning to emerge from scientific studies of complex systems. This
is a point to which we shall return.

A third concept of importance to Pannenberg is contingency.
This has two levels of meaning. One is purely metascientific, relating to an understanding of the world as ontologically dependent upon
its Creator in the manner already briefly alluded to in discussing
inertia. The second level concerns the openness of created process
to the future, so that cosmic history is seen to have the character of
an unfolding exploration, rather than the acting out of an already
determined scenario. Here the question of what can be learnt from
science about the causal nexus of the world is certainly relevant, even
if there must necessarily remain issues which will require metaphysical decision. A honest assessment of well-founded knowledge in this
respect shows that the scientific account is cloudy (because of intrinsic unpredictabilities present in both quantum theory and chaos
theory) and patchy (because of unresolved perplexities about how different regimes, such as the realm of quantum physics and the realm
of classical physics, in fact relate to each other). In characterising the
context of science, it is very important to acknowledge that it is not
currently able to offer a seamless account of the nature of physical
process, interpolating smoothly between the microphysics of the
subatomic world, the macrophysics of everyday happenings, and the
large-scale processes of cosmic history.[11] Certainly, an honest science
cannot deny to theology the metaphysical picture of a created uni-

verse open towards its future. This is another point to which we shall return.

Much more problematic to a scientist, and difficult to sustain, is Pannenberg's strongly expressed 'assumption of the priority of the future over past and present'.[12] The affirmation of the universe as a world of true becoming, which we shall discuss in chapter 3, implies that the future is as yet unformed and therefore the concept of its influence on the present becomes questionable. This is not to deny to God the teleological ability ultimately to bring about determined ends, even if by contingent paths,[13] but to decline to express this hope in terms of the image of a drawing-power acting from the future. Such talk seems an unnecessary paradoxical inversion of the concept of an unfolding divine purpose at work in creation.

The scientist-theologian will prefer the idea of God's ceaseless providential action, exercised in the moving present and within the open grain of created nature. The fact that quantum physics and thermodynamics both lead naturally to the concept of an arrow of time pointing unambiguously from past to future,[14] reinforces these reservations about laying an emphasis on the priority of the future. To borrow a musical metaphor from Arthur Peacocke, in the context of science cosmic history can best be seen as a great improvised fugue to which Creator and creatures both contribute, without denying that it will finally be brought to a divinely willed Resolution.[15]

Pannenberg has clearly made a serious effort to engage with modern science. The exercise has mostly been conducted at an elevated conceptual level, without a great deal of attention to the detailed content of science. As a result there has been a degree of conceptual misunderstanding, perhaps partly induced by too great a reliance on seeming verbal parallels involving the use of words such as 'field', which are supposed to encourage analogies that are, in fact, misleading. It is clear that there would have been benefit in conducting the engagement paying more attention to scientific style and content, in the manner that I am calling contextual.

Someone who has sought to look more closely at scientific content has been the Scottish Reformed theologian Thomas Torrance.[16] Yet his chosen heroes and guides, Michael Faraday, James Clerk Maxwell, and Albert Einstein, great scientists though they undoubtedly were, represent the final flowering of classical physics. The advent of modern quantum theory has meant that today we see them as the last of the Ancients rather than as the first of the Moderns. Torrance is eager, as surely all theologians ought to be, to dispel the notion that science's account of the universe is that of a closed and deterministic cosmos. However, he does not find the right way to defend his position. Once again the field concept is wrongly appealed to, as if by itself it relaxed the dead hand of mechanism. We have already seen that this is not the case, because of the deterministic character of classical fields. Ironically, Torrance thought that it was Einstein who found the way out of the deterministic prison, but in fact his whole approach to physics was based on the affirmation of a clear and determinate universe, since he wrongly believed that this was the only way to defend science's claim to a realistic knowledge of the physical world. In Einstein's thinking, realism was equated with unambiguous objectivity. Hence his well-known and life-long opposition to quantum theory in its modern form. Later we shall see how realism and openness can properly be defended in contemporary science.

Finally we must mention two theologians, the Jesuit Bernard Lonergan[17] and the Anglican Eric Mascall,[18] whose Thomistic thinking encouraged them to look for a positive relationship between faith and reason, theology and science. Both had sufficient mathematical ability to be able to engage with the specificities of physical theory. Their work represents a pioneering attempt at theology conducted in the context of science, in the form in which it could be formulated in the middle of the twentieth century. In the chapters that follow we shall look at the state of that project at the start of the twenty-first century.

2

Discourse

———◆◆◆———

The twentieth century saw a significant shift in the nature of discourse in the physical sciences. The physicists' earlier approach can be characterised as having depended upon a precise mathematical formulation of what, in its essential clarity and apparently deterministic order, was closely aligned to a commonsense way of thinking about what happens in the world. The detail of the scientific picture might change in unexpected ways, as when Copernicus's heliocentric system replaced the geocentric system of Ptolemy, but the basic style of argument and insight remained one in recognisable accord with ordinary human intuition. All that changed, as far as fundamental physics was concerned, in the first twenty-five years of the twentieth century.

Because of this fact that the clear and orderly world described by Isaac Newton and his successors was one whose general character did not contradict the perceived character of mundane experience, classical physics had not called for any radically counterintuitive manner of thought. The discovery of field theory in the nineteenth century did not significantly alter this state of affairs. Though the fields themselves were not objects that were directly visible, their effects were readily discernible, most graphically to be seen when scattered iron filings align themselves along the lines of force that Michael Faraday had brilliantly associated with a magnetic field. This state of affairs, corresponding to an unproblematic scientific discourse in a cousinly relationship to everyday thinking, radically changed in the early twentieth century with the discoveries of relativity and quantum theory. As the geneticist J. B. S. Haldane said in 1928, commenting on the work of his physicist colleagues, he had come to suspect that the universe was not only queerer than we had supposed, but queerer than we could have supposed. Under the prompting of the way that nature had actually turned out to behave, the physicists had been driven to discover entirely novel modes of thought.

Relativity theory abolished the seemingly natural Newtonian assumption of a universal and absolute experience of time, shared by all observers. This discovery will be a matter for discussion in the chapter that follows. Here we shall concentrate on the even more drastically revolutionary transformation of everyday thinking that quantum theory demanded.[1] It stems from the fundamental quantum assumption of the superposition principle. This basic quantum concept permits the combination of possibilities that commonsense would say could never be mixed together. An electron may be in a state where it is at a particular position, let us say 'here'. There is another state where it is somewhere else, say 'there'. In stark contrast to all Newtonian thinking and ordinary expectation, in quantum physics the electron can also be in states that are a superposition of these two possibilities, counterintuitive additions of 'here' and 'there'. The existence of such unpicturable states immediately implies the cloudy, unvisualisable character of the quantum world. Further analysis reveals that it also has to be a probabilistic world in which processess do not necessarily have determinate outcomes. If an actual measurement of position is made on a state which is a superposition of 'here' and 'there', sometimes the answer will be 'here' and sometimes the answer will be 'there'. The relative frequencies of obtaining these results are found to depend in a well-defined way upon the proportions in which the states of specific position make up the superposition, but no definite prediction can be made concerning which result will be obtained on any particular occasion of measurement.

Three further characteristics of quantum discourse derive from the superposition principle. Its implied cloudiness finds more precise expression in terms of Heisenberg's uncertainty principle. Classical physics posited the possibility of completely accurate knowledge of both a particle's position and its momentum. The experimentalist could determine both where it was and how it was moving. In quantum physics one may measure either position or momentum as accurately as one wishes, but one cannot do so for both simultaneously. If you know where an electron is, you cannot know what it is doing; if you know what it is doing, you cannot know where it is. Quantum epistemic access amounts to only half of that available in classical physics. All our thinking about the quantum world has to conform

14

to this limitation on knowledge. That world, therefore, can only be known in accordance with its Heisenbergian uncertainty and any attempt to demand Newtonian clarity is condemned to failure.

This result from physics illustrates a philosophical lesson of more general applicability. There is no universal epistemology applicable to all entities. They can only be known in a manner that conforms to their actual and individual natures. Different kinds of entities can be expected to be knowable in different kinds of ways. In relation to theology's search for knowledge of God, this point has been particularly emphasised by Thomas Torrance. He wrote, 'How God can be known must be determined from first to last by the way in which He actually is known.'[2] Theology practised in the context of science will certainly seek to follow this maxim.

A second consequence of the superposition principle is that a different logic applies to the quantum world, compared to that which operates in the everyday world. The latter was formulated by Aristotle and it depends upon the law of the excluded middle: there is no intermediate possibility between A and not-A. But we have seen that in the quantum world there is an infinite range of intermediate possibilities, corresponding to the different superpositions of A ('here') and not-A ('there'). Accordingly a more subtle form of what one may call quantum logic operates in that world.[3]

A third consequence of superposition arises from the fact that the intrinsic uncertainties of quantum physics allow entities to display in different circumstances quite different behaviours, of a kind that would be wholly incompatible with each other in classical physics, or according to commonsense understanding. The paradigm example is the well-known wave/particle duality of light, discovered as an empirical fact long before it could be theoretically understood. Ambidexterity of the wave/particle kind would be impossible in the clear world of Newtonian thinking, where a particle is small and concentrated, like a little bullet, and a wave is spread out and oscillatory, a flappy kind of thing. James Clerk Maxwell had identified light as waves propagating in the electromagnetic field but, much later, when quantum theory was applied to this field by Paul Dirac, it was found also to display particlelike properties. They arose because the characteristic effect of quantum mechanics is to transform quantities that classically can take any value in a given range (a continuous spectrum, as we say) into quantities that can take only specifically distinct values (a discrete spectrum). This is the physical property that produces sharp spectral lines in emissions from energetically excited atoms. It provides the basis for Max Planck's foundational insight that radiation does not ooze continuously out of a heated body, but it is emitted in discrete bundles of energy (quanta). It follows, therefore, that while a quantum field possess wavelike properties because of its extension in space and variation with time, its energy comes in discrete, countable packets, just like its being a collection of particles. Quantum field theory provides a clear and comprehensible example which shows how wave/particle duality is a coherent possibility. Analysis shows that wavelike states (technically, states with a definite phase) correspond to superpositions of different states containing different specific numbers of particles. In other words, a wavelike state corresponds to an indefinite number of particles, in the way that the superposition principle permits. This would be impossible classically, since in the clear light of day of the Newtonian world one would simply look and see exactly how many particles were present, and that would be that.

The strange and elusive nature of quantum entities has given rise to much argument about what degree of reality is to be attributed to them. Could it be that they are, as a positivist would suppose, no more than figments of the theoretical imagination, useful means for enabling stunningly accurate calculations to be made, but not to be taken with ontological seriousness? The great majority of physicists have resolutely resisted this suggestion. They take an instinctively realist view of what they learn through their investigation of the physical world. If science's discoveries were not revealing aspects of the actual nature of the universe, pure science would lose much of its motivation.[4] Of course, it is clear that the veiled character of the quantum world means that it does not enjoy the property of an unproblematic objectivity of a Newtonian kind. Quantum entities carry the potentiality for specific values of position or momentum, but at most they can only possess the actuality of one of these quantities. If quantum theory's idiosyncratic form of reality is to be defended, the best basis for the argument is an appeal to intelligibility as the ground for ontological belief. It is because belief in photons and electrons makes deep sense of a great swathe of directly observable phenomena, from the facts of chemistry to the properties of superconductors, that we affirm their reality. For similar reasons, particle physicists affirm the unseen reality of quarks, constituents of nuclear matter that are intrinsically unobservable, in the sense that they are believed to be 'confined', so tightly bound together that no one will ever succeed in detecting one existing on its own outside of the directly observable particles that the quarks are understood to constitute. Theology owes science no apology for its belief in the unseen reality of God, for that belief serves to make sense of great swathes of spiritual experience. An emphasis on the criterion of intelligibility as the key to ontology is strongly expressed in the Thomistic thinking of Bernard Lonergan, who speaks of God as 'the unrestricted act of understanding', the One whose existence and nature is the explanatory key to the character of created reality. Lonergan claims that 'the idea of being is the idea of the total range of intelligibility.'[5]

The epistemological stance that is adopted, consciously or unconsciously, by scientists can properly be called 'critical realism'. The noun expresses the conviction that the scientists are indeed exploring a physical world whose nature 'out there' is independent of human social construction (contra the allegations of many postmodern thinkers), while the adjective acknowledges that physical reality is often partly veiled and obliquely encountered (contra the expectation of simple objectivity that was entertained by the thinkers of the Enlightenment). Scientists do not believe themselves to be lost in a Kantian fog from which loom only the appearances of things (phenomena), with their true natures (noumena) remaining inaccessible. For them, epistemology (the knowledge of nature) is a reliable guide to ontology (the actual nature of things). The scientist-theologians agree in claiming that an analogous concept of critical realism appropriately describes theology's search for motivated belief arising from encounter with the veiled reality of God.[6]

We have been exploring how theology conducted in the context of science can benefit from analogies drawn from quantum physics. Of course there is no simplistic form of direct transfer between the two disciplines. The argument is certainly not that quantum physics is so strange that after it anything goes in other realms of discourse. That would be to make the crudest and least convincing move possible, by attempting to appeal to what one might dismissively term 'quantum hype'. What can be transferred, however, is rational encouragement to adopting an open and flexible mode of thought, responsive to the actually experienced character of reality, however unexpected that may prove to be. We have seen that everyday experience and commonsense expectation do not constitute a Procrustean bed into which all forms of rational discourse must be made to fit. Rather, the form of our thinking has to conform to the actual nature of what it is that we are seeking to think about. If quantum physics requires its idiosyncratic quantum logic, trinitarian theology may well require its own kind of logic also. If the quantum world cannot be known with a Newtonian clarity that assumes precise knowledge of both position and momentum, then maybe the assertions of apophatic theology – that there is an element of irreducible mystery involved in encounter with the infinite reality of God, beyond any finite human ability to articulate – should also be accorded appropriate respect. In every realm of human enquiry, well-winnowed experience should be taken with the utmost seriousness, even when its nature seems to run contrary to prior 'reasonable' expectation.

The phenomenon of wave/particle duality was known for more than twenty-five years before the discovery of quantum field theory dissolved its seeming threat of paradox. During that period, the physicists had no choice but to hold on to experience, even if it seemed contradictory to them. Here again theological parallels come readily to mind. The writers of the New Testament were driven to use both human and divine categories as they sought to express their experiences of the risen Christ, without being able to give a coherent reconciliation of the seeming paradox involved. Just as scientific understanding is propelled to new insight by the nudge of nature, so theological understanding is propelled by the nudge of encounter with divine reality.

Science succeeds in making comparatively rapid progress as it investigates a physical world which human beings transcend and which they can put to the experimental test. In theology the intellectual challenge, and the consequent timescale for progress, together with the partial character of what is achievable, is much greater, involving as it does the attempt to understand the infinite nature of the God who transcends finite humanity and who is properly to be met with in awe and trust, properly declining to be put to crude empirical testing of an attempted manipulative kind. Nevertheless, one should recognise that the apparent paradoxes that face Christian theology – the duality of divinity and humanity in Jesus Christ; the triune nature of the one true God – have not arisen by way of free-wheeling metaphysical speculation, but through attempts to wrestle with the historical testimony of the New Testament and the worshipping experience of the Church. Theologians who practise in the context of science can take encouragement from their scientific colleagues to accord primacy to carefully evaluated experience. Even if its character seems disturbingly perplexing and unexpected, they should not let that tempt them to set it aside. If the physical world has proved queerer than we supposed, or could have supposed, it would scarcely seem strange if the same were true of that world's Creator. We shall return to this theme in chapter 6.

The often surprising character of the physical world gives science much of its excitement. One never knows what may be lying in wait around the next experimental corner. It also means that the instinctive question for a scientist to ask about a novel proposal is not 'Is it reasonable?', for no one in 1899 could have considered quantum theory to be reasonable. Any first-year philosophy student could have 'proved' the impossibility of wave/particle duality. Human powers of rational prevision are decidedly myopic. Even Max Planck, who in 1900 had made the first tentative step towards a new kind of physics by suggesting that radiation might be emitted and absorbed in discrete quanta, spoke later of how dissatisfied he had been with this venturesome proposal, notwithstanding its immediate success in solving a perplexing problem by determining correctly the spectrum of black body radiation. In consequence of nature's frequent refusal to conform to prior expectation, the natural question for a scientist to ask about a novel suggestion is 'What makes you think that might be the case?' The form of the question is open-minded in not attempting to impose a prior constraint on the form of an acceptable answer, but it is also stringent in insisting on being given evidence for whatever understanding is being proposed.

If theology is to be conducted persuasively and successfully in the context of science, it must be prepared to respond to this kind of interrogation. My belief is that answering appropriately calls for the kind of theological style that I have called 'bottom-up thinking.'[7] The strategy required is one that seeks to move from motivating experience to attained understanding. An evidence-based approach of this kind contrasts with 'top-down thinking', which attempts to start from supposed general principles and then descend to the consideration of particulars. At the time of the Enlightenment, the Cartesian programme of basing knowledge on the sure foundation of clear and certain ideas essayed just such an ambitious top-down strategy. It is not without its aspirants in philosophical theology today. Top-down argument is an intellectually attractive prospect, but too often it has proved to be a mirage, as the proposed foundational ideas turn out not to possess the clarity or the certainty that had been assumed. The humbler approach of bottom-up argument is the better way to proceed. No one could have discovered quantum theory by means of top-down argument. It needed the irresistible nudge of nature to push physicists in the counterintuitive direction of the superposition principle. Seeking to do justice to scriptural testimony to the revelatory acts of God in history drove the Church to trinitarian and incarnational thinking. The essence of rationality is to strive to conform one's thinking to the nature of what is being thought about, and this means that different domains of encounter with reality will require their specifically different forms of rational expression. The tendency among atheist writers to identify reason exclusively with scientific modes of thought is a disastrous diminishment of our human powers of truth-seeking enquiry.

Recognition that theology is concerned in its proper domain with the search for truth attainable through motivated belief rebuts the assertion sometimes made by the more strident members of the atheist community, that theology does not deserve a place in the modern academy since, they alledge, it is not a truly intellectually open-minded pursuit. The reality of the matter is completely the reverse. A university that does not have a faculty of theology is incomplete, since it fails to engage with the widely attested human experience of encounter with the sacred dimension of reality.[8]

I strongly believe that it is possible to do theology in a bottom-up fashion and that its pursuit in the context of science will indeed require just this kind of approach. In my Gifford Lectures I sought to explore and defend statements drawn from the Nicene Creed, framing the argument along exactly such lines.[9] For example, it was necessary to consider as carefully and as scrupulously as possible the motivation for the Christian belief that Jesus was raised from the dead on the third day, to live a new life of everlasting glory. This required an assessment of what historical reality might lie behind the New Testament stories of the appearances of the risen Christ and the discovery of the empty tomb. It also required consideration of whether there is an understanding of the nature of God, and of created reality, that could coherently accommodate belief in the resurrection without such belief seeming to imply accepting Easter as the act of an arbitrary celestial Conjurer. (The theological problem of miracle is essentially the problem of discerning divine consistency, preserved in the face of claims for the occurrence of unprecedented events.)[10] My conclusion was, and remains, that it is possible to affirm well-motivated and theologically coherent belief in Christ's resurrection, and in fact my Christian faith and understanding turns on that belief. I shall return to this point in chapter 6, but I want now to emphasise that something like this kind of rational discourse is indispensable for any adequate attempt to do theology in the context of science. In particular, theology has to take issues of the reliability of historical testimony very seriously. The Bible is not to be treated as if it were an infallible, divinely dictated, textbook, but rather as the indispensable record of divine revelatory acts made in the course of the unfolding history of Israel and the unique phenomenon of Jesus Christ.

Scientists know that there are no really interesting scientific facts that are not already interpreted facts. This is an issue to which we shall return shortly. For the moment, it is sufficient to note that the resulting subtlety required in the character of scientific argument is such that it should make it easy for scientists to recognise that the scrupulous evaluation of biblical evidence is also something much more delicate than simply treating the gospels as if they were just unproblematic pieces of detached and matter-of-fact reporting. The evangelists are seeking to convey a certain religious conviction to their readers, expressed by means of interpreted accounts of incidents in the life of Jesus Christ. They offer interpretations that point to timeless truths, yet this does not mean that the gospels are simply mythic tales, unanchored in any form of actual occurrence. Christianity should welcome the challenge to exhibit and evaluate its evidential foundations. The religion of the incarnation is based on the claim that its myth of the Word made flesh is an enacted myth and not simply a moving symbolic story. This means that theology should be happy to operate in the questioning context of science.

Such an evidence-based approach to theological understanding bears a readily discernible cousinly relationship to scientific reasoning. Elsewhere, I have given a detailed point-by-point comparison of thinking in quantum physics and in Christian theology, analysed along exactly these lines.[11] Of course, there is not an identity between the two methods of enquiry, and it is instructive to consider both the similarities and the differences that there are between them.

While both disciplines appeal to evidence, the character of that evidence is notably different in the two cases. Whenever possible, science deals with general and repeatable processes, exploring situations that can be replicated at will. The impersonal character of the events with which science deals mostly enables them to be investigated in this way, repeating the enquiry as frequently as may be considered necessary. This ability gives science its great secret weapon of experiment, and so it affords it ready access to the strength of conviction that successful empirical appeal can produce. If one does not accept the assertions of one's colleagues then, at least in principle and quite often in practice, one can go and look for oneself. It is not necessary simply to rely on the testimony of others. However, even in science this power of repetition is not quite universally true. The historico-observational sciences, such as physical cosmology and evolutionary biology, do not share in the general scientific ability to contrive at will special situations for investigation. There is a unique history of the universe, and a unique history of terrestrial life. These are simply given and they have to be understood on the basis of the fragmentary evidence that is available about them. More evidence cannot be produced at will by direct human manipulation. When new observations do become available, such as may arise from recognising the existence of neutron stars or from fresh discoveries of fossil remains, they come to the scientist as unsolicitable gifts. Advance of understanding in the observational sciences has to arise from inferring to the best explanation of those significant events of which science has had the good fortune to gain a partial knowledge.

In most other forms of human experience, the personal element that is involved removes any possibility for unrestricted repetition. We do not hear a Mozart quartet the same way twice, even if we play the same disc on each occasion. Human encounter with the transpersonal reality of God is irreducibly unique in its character. Any effort to manipulate the divine in order to induce repeated effects is simply to commit the sinful error of attempting magic. Christian theology depends critically on testimony relating to the unique history of Israel and the uniquely significant episode of the life, death, and resurrection of Jesus Christ. Of course, the insights thus conveyed must find some correlation with the individual experiences of the believer and the corporate experiences of Christian communities, and conversely Christian understanding is delivered from mere subjective reliance on the feelings of pious individuals precisely by those experiences being subject to evaluation in the light of the foundational revelatory events and by their being assessed within the truth-seeking community of the Church.

The necessary role of the unique in theology can sometimes be a stumbling block for scientists. Their professional stance is one of reliance on generality, and this can make them unduly wary of the particular. Yet physicists are also persons and they should reflect how arid life would be if conducted on the premise that only experiences and understandings that are open to boundless repetition could be of real significance. No one living a human life can escape from the ambiguity and rich uniqueness inherent in personal encounter.

Sometimes people try to draw a distinction between the discourses of science and theology by alleging that the former deals with facts but the latter merely with opinions. Two errors are contained in this assertion. First, we have already noted that there are no scientific 'facts' of any interest that are not already interpreted facts. Mere instrumental registrations are of no significance unless one also knows what it is that the apparatus is capable of measuring. Deciding what this is requires reliance on theoretical opinion. That is why measurements and their meanings, experiment and theory, inextricably intertwine in subtle ways in scientific thinking.[12] This mutuality gives a certain air of precarious circularity to scientific argument, but the fruitful and continuing explanatory success that science achieves strongly suggests that this circularity is benign and not vicious. Even in the face of postmodernist criticism, I believe that science is right to claim verisimilitudinous understanding as its epistemic attainment.[13]

The philosopher of science who I believe has offered the most helpful account of the method and achievement of science is Michael Polanyi, who was able in his thinking to draw upon long experience of working as a distinguished physical chemist.[14] Polanyi understood science to be necessarily an activity of persons, since its pursuit calls for the exercise of tacit skills of judgement about experimental interpretation (such as the successful elimination of the spurious effects of unwanted 'background' events) and theoretical evaluation (successful theories, although consistent with experiment, are never simply read out of experimental findings, but their discovery requires also the exercise of creative imagination). The relevant procedures cannot simply be written down in a manual of technique, but they have to be learnt through apprenticeship in a truth-seeking community. While science is thus a form of personal quest for knowledge, nevertheless its practice is carried out with universal intent and within the controlling context of the actual nature of the physical world. In *Personal Knowledge*, Polanyi tells us that he wrote the book in order to explain how, as a scientist, he could commit himself to what he believed to be true, while knowing that it might be false.

I believe this to be the status of all human knowledge. We are able to attain best explanations of our experience, which we should treat with the utmost seriousness, but to claim to have achieved absolute proof and indubitable certainty is to go beyond finite human capacity. Absolutely coercive argument is not at our disposal. The context of science is a context of the attainment of persuasive insight to which we may rationally commit ourselves, rather than the achievement of unrevisable certainty. Reason is not to be identified with the possession of indisputable proof, but with the careful search for well-motivated belief, whether we are concerned with science or with theology. We have seen that even mathematics is qualified by Gödel's discovery that axiomatised systems cannot determine their own consistency and, if consistent, they contain true statements that cannot be proved within the system itself. Mathematical truth, it seems, exceeds the rational certainties available through exhaustive analysis. Realisation that this is the case should induce epistemic humility, but it should not bring about epistemic paralysis. Personal knowledge simply requires a degree of intellectual commitment and daring. Theology, of course, shares in this common need to be at once modest and bold in the search for understanding. The fact that in its own quest theology seeks to make appeal to motivated belief shows that it was a bad error to suggest that it trades only in airy opinions. Bottom-up thinking in theology does not claim a fideistic certainly that is beyond all possibility of intellectual challenge, but rather it strives to attain rational justification for its beliefs. In that sense, the theologian truly lives by (motivated) faith and not by (certain) sight. Of course, what is true of religious belief is also true of atheism. There is a certain tendency in contemporary society to treat atheism as if it were the natural default position, with the burden of argument resting solely with theists. This is not the case. Everyone has a metaphysical position or world view, and each such view is in need of metaphysical argument in its defence. The proper stance of believers with respect to atheists is not that they are stupid in declining to see things in a religious way – for it is very clearly the case that many atheists are people of high intelligence and have a sincere desire for truth – but simply that, in fact, theism offers a more comprehensive understanding than atheism can. An example of what might be said in defence of that claim would be the suggestion that the deep intelligibility of the universe – the fact that actually makes science possible but which science itself is unable to explain – is not a mere happy accident, but it is a sign that the Mind of the Creator lies behind the wonderful order that scientists are privileged to explore. We shall return to this theme in chapter 4.

Polanyi's emphasis on the necessity of commitment to belief in science, which is such a strong theme in his writings, makes it clear how misleading it would be to claim, as people sometimes do, that scientists are sceptics, always prepared to doubt everything. Such an unrelenting strategy of universal doubt would be destructive of the possibility of gaining understanding. In pursuing the quest for truth one has to be willing to accept gratefully, if not uncritically, the heritage of the past. Isaac Newton was willing to say that in making his great discoveries he had been able to see further because he had stood on the shoulders of giants. Of course, respect for one's predecessors does not mean being totally in thrall to past ideas, as if credulity were to be commended and corrigibility excluded. Galileo was right about the Earth's motion, but mistaken about the nature of the tides. Ideas change and revisions become necessary, but usually one can detect a thread of continuity linking the present to the past, even in periods of quite drastic change. After Einstein, Newton was not seen as simply being wrong, but rather the limits of the validity of his ideas had been made apparent. Classical mechanics is still good enough to send an explorer satellite to Mars. The pioneers of quantum theory had to develop what they called 'correspondence principles', showing how the successful results of classical physics could be recovered in those regimes where it served as a good approximation to the nature of physical process.

Theology in its turn has no need to resist being open to development and correction in the light of further insight and understanding. Neither the Nicene doctrine of the Trinity, nor the Chalcedonian definition of the two natures of Christ, is clearly articulated in the pages of the New Testament. These understandings came later, and the character of the insight that they have to offer lies in indicating the kind of thinking that has been found to be consonant with the Church's experience, rather than presenting a detailed prescription for the absolutely final shape that thinking must take. What one does find in the New Testament are accounts of the foundational Christian experiences, reflection on which led the Church, after centuries of theological argument and exploration, to formulate these counterintuitive doctrines. Theological engagement with trinitarian insight did not come to an end in 381 at the Council of Constantinople, nor did Christology attain its final form in 451 at the Council of Chalcedon. Exploration of these profound Christian themes has continued down the centuries, as might be expected by those who believe in the development of doctrine taking place under the guidance of the Holy Spirit. Sometimes previous ideas have had to be abandoned completely. The attempt to understand the atoning work of Christ in terms of the theory of 'the deceiver deceived' (the crudely expressed notion that the devil was defeated at Calvary because he was led into attempting illegitimately to assert rights over the sinless Christ), which had been proposed by Origen in the third century and which was received and accepted by a number of the Church Fathers in the centuries that followed, is today recognised as being grotesquely inadequate as an attempt to understand the nature of Christ's victory over the power of evil.

The difficulty of its task makes the rate of change of thinking in theology slower than it is in science, but this by no means implies that that discipline is in thrall to past ideas which it is unable in any respect to modify or even repudiate. Theology is a truth-seeking enterprise, and when it is conducted in a context of science it is liable to see particularly clearly the need to be open to correction and change. Nevertheless, I believe that doctrinal development takes place best in a continuous relationship of dialogue with the past. Theology too has need of its own correspondence principles.[15]

Active dialogue across the centuries is particularly important for theology because the rich profundity of its subject material means that it has to be especially careful not to lose the insights of other epochs. For example, it may well be that the English mystics of the fourteenth century, such as Julian of Norwich and the unknown author of *The Cloud of Unknowing*, had access to experience and possessed powers of discernment that are of great significance, and which we in the twenty-first century will be able to profit from only if we are willing to apprentice ourselves to their experience and understanding. Theology is intrinsically a diachronic subject; its discourse has to span the centuries. Augustine and Aquinas, Luther and Calvin, are enduring participants in the theological conversation. Science is different. The comparatively tractable character of its subject matter enables its discourse to be synchronic. Physicists today do not need to read the *Principia*, since its many insights of lasting value are uncontroversially incorporated into contemporary textbooks. Scientific knowledge accumulates in a straightforwardly linear manner. A physicist today knows much more about the universe than Newton ever did, simply by virtue of living three centuries later than that great genius. Theology is not cumulative in this unproblematic way. There is no presumptive superiority of present-day theologians over those of earlier centuries.

It is both possible and fruitful to conduct theology in the context of science, not because these two forms of the search for truthful understanding are without significant differences from each other, but because underlying their surface distinctions there is a common sharing in openness to reality which makes them intellectual cousins under the skin. Theology and science are partners in the human quest for truth and understanding, gained through the search for motivated belief. The character of their mutual engagement must reflect this fact.

Finally there is a second mode of discourse that must also be considered. Contextual theologies often lay stress on a specific approach to ethical issues, corresponding to the particular concerns and experiences that relate to their constituency. Liberation theology speaks powerfully of the moral imperative of an 'option for the poor'. Black theology maintains a resolute resistance to racial discrimination.

Feminist theology stresses opposition to gender stereotyping and the disempowerment of women.

In the context of science, many important and difficult ethical issues arise from the need to discern the right and wrong uses of the novel forms of technical power that scientific advance continually makes available. A distinction must be made between pure science's quest for knowledge, which is surely always desirable when pursued by ethically acceptable means, since knowledge is a better basis for decision than ignorance could ever be, and technology's use of that knowledge to create the power to get things done. The latter is a much more ambiguous gift, since not everything than can be done should be done. An extensive literature has been devoted to the discussion of these issues.[16] Yet science's self-defining abstention from considering questions of value means that, strictly understood, the context of science does not afford the means for dealing with these problems. The ethical issues concerned have arisen from the possibility of exploiting the opportunities offered by science, but science itself does not provide the insights that are needed to make the necessary acts of moral judgement. Scientists, as scientists, can give factual information about the general character of natural processes, and they can endeavour to estimate the possible consequences of interventions in nature that might be undertaken with the hope of manipulating circumstances to human advantage. Whatever the matter under consideration may be – whether a new therapeutic procedure in medicine, or the environmentally perturbing effects of industrial processes – the scientists' carefully considered predictions of what is likely to happen are certainly an indispensable contribution to the setting in which to make an ethical evaluation of what is proposed. Yet these predictions do not themselves constitute that evaluation. The context of science is the context of possible results, but of itself it does not provide the ethical setting within which these results can be morally assessed. That lies elsewhere. Making the right decisions about technological exploitation is the concern of ethically responsible society at large. Once they have given their predictions of likely consequences, the scientists participate in the debate simply as citizens. They certainly cannot aspire to be treated as sole judges in their own cause.

In view of this restricted role for purely scientific insights in reaching ethical decisions, our discussion will be brief, concerning itself simply with some observations about science's influence on the attitude with which society approaches questions relating to the use of technological resources, rather than attempting to give a detailed survey of some of the many individual ethical decisions that actually have to be made.[17]

A classic way of making the distinction between what science can offer and what it would be ethically right to do with them is to discriminate 'what is' (including the possibilities inherent in physical and biological research and the nature of the consequences likely to arise from their exploitation) from 'what ought to be' (the moral judgement of what it is right to permit to happen). In considering moral decision-making, it is important to recognise that the natural and the ethical are not at all identical, and the distinction between what is naturally occuring and what requires human contrivance is not of itself of moral significance. A great deal of medical practice is radically unnatural, as the case of heart transplants makes clear enough. The argument that the use of a particular scientific technique would be a step too far in human presumption – an attempt to 'play God' as the phrase goes – requires in itself very careful evaluation. Human beings are a part of created nature and they have been given their gifts in order to use them responsibly. Of course, not everything that can be done, should be done, but the natural/unnatural distinction is not the criterion by which the necessary ethical discrimination can be made.

Moral wisdom certainly does not require a resistance to change. As evolutionary insight makes clear, there is no warrant for believing that a static creation is the divine intention. The only state that is totally static is death. In fact, in terrestrial history, the great periods of the fruitful diversification of life arose following periods of widespread extinction. Yet reckless change is not desirable either, and the fact that current human activity is reducing biodiversity through an extinction rate at least a thousand times greater than the natural rate, is not one that we should regard with complacency or ethical indifference.

Many ethical dilemmas arise from the difficulty of striking a right balance between achievable good and unavoidable harm. The choice offered is seldom one between black and white, but varying shades of grey. For example, in medicine few therapies are free from undesirable side effects. One must be prepared to ask what degree of the prolongation of life justifies the cost, in terms of the patient's endurance and the use of limited resources, of some new and intense form of chemotherapy. That is not a question whose answer is quantifiable in terms of the objective criteria of medical science alone. The need for a subtle wisdom in seeking moral judgements is frequently disguised by the nature of much of what passes for ethical discussion in contemporary society. The character of current discourse is often that of the clash of single-issue pressure groups, one claiming that 'X is wonderful, let's get on with it'; the other that 'X is terrible, don't even think of it'. Whatever X may be, it is very unlikely that either of these statements is true. X may be beneficial in some circumstances, harmful in others. Radiation, which can be highly damaging in many situations, can also, in a totally different setting, provide an acceptable means to improve the bacteriological safety of food. In seeking to strike a balance between benefit and harm it is important to recognise that, while the factual context of scientific assessment can provide a helpful analysis of likely consequences, it is very seldom in a position to offer an absolute asssurance of the total safety of a novel process.

A further perplexity that is beyond a purely scientific ability to resolve can arise from the need for metaphysical acts of judgement in assessing moral status. At present there is a good deal of controversy about the ethical propriety of research involving human embryos. There is a general consensus among medical ethicists that humans are always ends and never means, so that interventions on them should be with the consent of, and for the benefit of, the individual patient concerned. But how does this principle relate to the very early embryo? It is clearly human life, but is it already a full human person? Medical scientists can tell us that before fourteen days of development (at which time the primitive streak begins to appear) the embryo has no structure beyond that of the DNA in each of its undifferentiated cells. Until that time, it is even capable of spontaneous division into two embryos, leading to identical twins. What the medical scientists, as scientists, cannot tell us is whether that early embryo really is already a full human person, with the absolute moral status that would attach to that. This is a question whose answer lies outside the province of science, and it can only be addressed by recourse to acts of metaphysical and theological insight and judgement. I have suggested that whether one takes a dualist or a psychosomatic view of human nature is likely to influence the form that this judgement takes, since the latter position encourages taking the developmental view that personhood is something that is grown into, while the former position is consistent with, and may well encourage, seeing personhood as being bestowed at conception by the divine gift of a spiritual soul.[18]

The context of science raises ethical problems, but it does not determine their solutions. Yet in quite another way, science can have some general influence on the intellectual climate within which such solutions may be sought. This arises from its account of a world wonderfully ordered and stupendously fertile. Though science does not use the language of value, it describes a world to which it seems perfectly natural to assign the concept of its intrinsic worth. In the ancient words of Genesis 1 (vv. 4, 10, 12, 18, 21, 25, 31) the creation is fittingly seen to be 'good'. Such fruitfulness should not wantonly be destroyed by human exploitation for selfish ends. If there is an ethical slogan fit for use in the context of science, it would surely be an 'option for nature', expressing a concept of ecological respect.

It is ironic that the very same chapter of scripture to which I have just referred is also the one which, through its motif of 'dominion' (vv. 26 and 28), has been seen as having given licence to the human ravaging of nature.[19] It is certainly the case that Christian thinkers such as Francis Bacon and René Descartes – both incidently influential in the development of modern science – expressed strongly their belief in a God-given right for human beings to be unhesitating in exploiting natural processes to their advantage. However, contemporary exegetes prefer to temper the notion of absolute kingly dominion by recalling the Israelite ideal of the shepherd king, responsible for the welfare of all his flock. One must remember also that in the older creation story of Genesis 2, Adam is given the task of tilling and keeping the garden that God had planted (v. 15). This horticultural image encourages taking an environmentally responsible attitude toward nature. A gardener must exercise a degree of control over nature, for otherwise weeds will choke all other forms of plant life, but the gardener has also to respect and work within the given grain of nature. No gardener can grow rhododendra in an alkaline soil.

In chapter 4, I shall suggest that science of itself, while providing some insights from evolutionary biological thinking, is unable to offer an intelligible and fully adequate explanation of the origin of our ethical intuitions. There is an irreducible character to moral value which clearly distinguishes radical altruism from simply prudential strategies for genetic propagation. Theology in the context of science will recognise the importance of the many ethical issues that arise from the ever-increasing expansion of technical possibilities offered by the advance of science, but it will have to look to its own resources to find the necessary wisdom to respond to the challenges that these discoveries present.

3

Time and space

It is almost a convention to begin theological reflection on the nature of time by recalling Augustine's famous remark in the *Confessions* that until he came to think about it he knew what time was, but once he began to reflect on its nature he became perplexed. Scientists too are not without puzzlement when it comes to speaking about the nature of time. Nevertheless, they have some insights into temporality that can be offered, and that are worth thinking about. Yet, these gifts from science do not always seem to be taken fully into account by the theologians. Some of the matters of concern are quantitative and some are qualitative. We shall take the quantitative first.

One of the most important scientific discoveries made in the course of the past two centuries has been that of the existence of 'deep time', the immense span of gradually unfolding process that has brought into being the form of the present. Recognition of this fact was first gained in geology and then continued in other sciences, as people slowly became aware of the immense timescales involved in terrestrial and cosmic history. Today we know that the Earth is about 4.5 billion years old and the observable universe has an age of 13.7 billion years. Over these vast aeons, the nature of the universe and the nature of the Earth were subject to many changes. A universe that had begun as an almost uniform expanding ball of energy came to contain within it the home of saints and scientists. The timescales implied by the sacred texts of the three Abrahamic faiths are measured only in thousands of years, as is the whole recorded history of human culture, although the creation myths of the Eastern religions do invoke the idea of very much longer epochs. If the age of the universe were taken to correspond to a single cosmic 'Year', then the time from Abraham to the present day would amount to less than the final ten seconds of the last 'Day'.

33

Of course theologians are aware of these facts, but they do not always seem to take them with sufficient seriousness. If theology is to function successfully in the context of science, it will need to pay more heed to scientific insight into cosmic timescales. The argument is certainly not that the significance of all periods of the universe's history is simply to be measured by their chronological length. Size and significance are undoubtedly not the same thing, as the importance that the cosmologists assign to the universe's history in the first three minutes following the big bang makes clear enough.[1] That brief primaeval era saw a succession of hectic changes, at the end of which the present character of the forces of nature had been established and the gross nuclear structure of the cosmos was fixed. A succeeding period of about a billion years saw the much slower process of the formation of the first stars and galaxies. Life would not appear for about nine more billion years. The timescales of creation should at least encourage in the theological mind the thought that the Creator is not a God in a hurry. It is also highly questionable that the final fulfilment of the present creation is to be expected in the comparatively near future. Scientific expectations stretch forward over periods of time very much greater than that which has already elapsed since the big bang. Their predicted character is not ultimately encouraging to any simple notion of final fulfilment. If present process simply continues, eventually all carbon-based life will disappear from the cosmos, whose end will lie in futility, most probably resulting from the ever-increasing cold and relentless decay of a universe that will continue to expand. When theologians speak of the future, they need to take account of these predictions, yet their thinking often seems to be confined at most to the next few thousand years. This particular point is one to which we shall return in chapter 7.

An associated problem for theological discussion is the ultimacy of the status of human beings. In an evolving world, the average lifetime of any one species is only a few million years (though those who populate a well-protected niche, such as that which the turtles have exploited, can do distinctly better than that). On the other hand, the doctrine of the incarnation implies a unique significance for humanity. In the following chapter I shall argue that the development of hominids represented the emergence of a radically new form of being, but one might ask whether this was not just the first stage of a long process, and might not human beings be expected to have successors with capacities that exceed those of homo sapiens as greatly as our capacities exceed those of the dinosaurs? It is difficult to know how to answer these questions, because the dawning of self-consciousness has radically modified the character of evolutionary process as far as humanity is concerned. Compassion and medical science mean that the unfit are not simply left to die. Written culture affords a method of transmitting information from one generation to the next which is vastly more effective than that of differential genetic propagation. These distinctive developments have been operating only for periods that are very short on a evolutionary timescale, and it is consequently hard to evaluate what they imply for the future.

A degree of parochiality in theological talk is also apparent in relation to spatial scale. When theologians talk about 'the world', their meaning is usually the immediate human locality of planet Earth. Yet the Sun is a pretty ordinary star among the hundred thousand million stars of our galaxy, the Milky Way, and the Milky Way itself is a pretty ordinary galaxy among the hundred thousand million galaxies of the observable universe. Science's understanding of the immense extent of the cosmos is even more difficult to take in on a human scale than are the vast aeons of cosmic time. We human beings are the inhabitants of a mere speck of cosmic dust. Once again, however, size and significance are not necessarily at all the same thing. In fact, a universe that was much smaller than ours would not have lasted long enough to have been able to evolve carbon-based life of our kind of complexity. In a real sense, all that vast multitude of stars is necessary for the possibility of our being here as the inhabitants of Earth.

It is natural to go on to ask, 'Are there living beings elsewhere in this vast cosmos?' Attempting to answer this question is difficult. Because we do not yet understand the processes by which life developed, the problem is that we do not know how hard it is for it actually to happen. Life certainly requires a very specific kind of planetary environment. Suitable temperatures and appropriate chemical resources are obviously necessary, but on their own they are unlikely to be enough. For example, it is believed that an important factor enabling the development of terrestrial life has been the existence of the Moon, an unusually large satellite in relation to the size of its planet, the Earth. The Moon's presence has not only stabilised the rotation of the Earth, thereby avoiding sharp climatic changes that would have put developing life at risk, but it has also induced strong tides which scoured vital mineral resources from the land and poured them into the sea, the place where life is likely to have begun. Yet there are so many stars in the universe, many of which are believed to have planetary systems, that surely there must be many potential sites available for life to develop, however exacting the requirements. However, there are unresolved disputes among the experts about how probable that process of biogenesis is likely to be. Some say that the development of life is almost inevitable given the appropriate circumstances,[2] while others claim that it seems so hard to understand how it occurred once that the possibility of it happening several times is extremely remote.[3] Those of us who are not biologists must conclude that the question of the likelihood of extraterrestrial life, and even more of extraterrestrial intelligence, remains for the present an open one.

Theologians would be wise to be prepared for either answer. They should consider whether there is any pressing reason to suppose that the divine creative and salvific intentions focus on homo sapiens alone. Might they not also include 'little green men', if such there be? God's creative generosity surely does not need to be construed in a narrow fashion.[4] This issue has in fact been debated by theologians ever since Galileo made it plain (contrary to Aristotle) that the heavens are made of the same sort of materials as the Earth. People began to speculate that there might be Martians or Venusians and to ask, if so, did Christ die for them as well as for us? Two different responses were made. One claimed that it was sufficient for the Son of God to assume creaturely life somewhere for the whole of creation thereby to be redeemed, even if this implied that the Martians and Venusians might not actually know about it. The other response suggested that if there were other creatures in need of redemption, the Word would have taken their flesh also, just as he had taken ours. While repeated acts of incarnation in the same rational species might be considered an unacceptable or incoherent notion, it is not clear that this is true of incarnation in different kinds of rational being. Despite a certain theological logic attaching to the first response, I incline to the second, since I believe that God is generous, not only in love but also in self-disclosure.

The qualitative issues that arise for a theology conducted in the context of science focus principally on the nature of time. For the scientist, the philosopher and the theologian alike, space seems to be an altogether less problematic concept. No doubt this is partly because we have the ability to move around in space, while time-travel is not within our capacity. Yet one has to say that it is not absolutely clear that the notion of measuring rods, capable of metricating space, is more straightforward than the notion of standard clocks, capable of metricating time. General relativity, of course, intimately connects space and time together as they bend under the influence of matter, producing a curvature which in its turn deflects the paths of material particles, an effect which is the modern understanding of the nature of gravity. For the relativist, space, time, and matter form a single, integrated system. However, this by no means implies a simple equivalence between space and time. History remains different from geography. Another contrast between the character of our experiences of space and time lies in the fact that in space we have the ability to stand still, but this is denied us in the case of time, whose steady progression cannot be halted. In fact, it is just the seemingly relentlessly unfolding character of our experience of temporal process, giving rise to the idea of a developing history, that makes the nature of time seem so much more problematic than the natures of space and matter. Before considering the issues relating to temporality, two important preliminary points need to be made.

The first is that we shall see that the nature of time turns out to be a metaphysical question, whose answer is constrained by science, but not fully settled by it. How scientific discoveries are interpreted in forming a metaphysical world view depends on the metascientific convictions of the interpreter. Consequently, it is a perfectly proper possibility for theological considerations to play their part in decisions relating to the adoption and defence of a particular account of temporality. The context of science does not of itself provide a complete determination of what that view should be. We shall find in chapter 4 that the same is true of causality.

The second point to be made is that the question of the nature of time and the question of the nature of causality (deterministic or indeterministic, for example) are quite separate metaphysical issues. The answer given to one does not imply that a specific answer has to be given to the other. Causality relates to the nature of the interconnection of events, whether deterministic or open in character, and this can find appropriate expression whatever view is taken of the nature of the time within which those events are located.

In Newtonian thinking, absolute time and absolute space furnished the universal setting within which dynamical processes took place. Einstein's theory of special relativity abolished both these absolutes. Different observers will experience and describe space and time in different ways. Yet absolutes remain, though of a different kind. They are the speed of light, which the theory states will be the same for all observers, and a quantity called interval, a kind of 'distance' in the four-dimensional continuum of space-time, on which all observers will agree. The existence of these invariants enables a consistent reconciliation of the accounts given by different observers. In particular, the causal ordering of related events will be the same for all observers. If an event B is caused by event A, then B must lie in the forward lightcone of A (that is, the domain of space-time bounded by light rays emitted from A; the backward lightcone of A is the domain bounded by light rays that impinge on A). This is because causally effective information cannot propagate faster than light.[5] Lightcones are invariant domains, the same for all observers, and so all observers will agree about causal ordering. Einstein's general theory of relativity, representing gravitational effects in terms of space-time curvature, involves a more complex four-dimensional space-time geometry, but it exhibits essentially similar properties.

Two relativistic effects are of particular interest for theology in the context of science. One is that different observers experience the rate of the passage of time in different ways, according to their states of motion. A traditional way of expressing this effect is to say that moving clocks run slow compared to a stationary clock. A picturesque consequence is the so-called 'twin paradox'. One twin stays stationary on Earth, while the other shoots off and back again in a fast spaceship. When they meet once more, the travelling twin will be found to be younger than the Earth-bound twin, because his moving body-clock has been ticking more slowly. While the effect is counterintuitive, it is not a real paradox, since the twins' experiences are different (one goes on a journey and the other does not) and there is no reason why the final consequences for them should not be different also. Abundant experimental evidence (not involving actual twins, of course, but relating to the observed decay times of unstable particles) has accumulated to confirm the correctness of this prediction of special relativity.

The second relativistic effect that is of interest is that different observers will make different judgements concerning the simultaneity or otherwise of distant events. To understand how this comes about, consider the following situation. A spaceship is passing close to an observer on Earth. At the moment of passing, a light flash is emitted from a source at the centre of the ship. An observer travelling with the ship will judge this light to be reflected simultaneously in two mirrors at the opposite ends of the ship, since it has the same distance to travel in either direction. The observer on Earth, however, will reach a different conclusion. He will judge it to be reflected in the stern mirror before it is reflected in the bow mirror. This is because the motion of the ship while the flash of light is travelling brings the stern nearer and the bow farther away from the earthling who, since the speed of light is the same for him as it is for the traveller on the ship, will conclude that the flash hit the stern mirror before it hit the bow mirror. A little thought will show that this difference will only be readily apparent if the spaceship is travelling relative to the Earth at a significant fraction of the velocity of light (approximately three hundred thousand kilometres a second).

The relative character of the simultaneity of distant events has been invoked as an argument in favour of the theory of what is called the block universe, the assertion that the true reality is the atemporal state comprising the four-dimensional totality of cosmic space-time, and that the contrary belief in the reality of a moving present is simply a trick of psychological perspective on the part of human beings as they track along their paths (world-lines) through the space-time continuum.[6] Einstein was a firm believer in the block universe point of view, even seeking to console the widow of an old friend by the thought that the past and future are essentially as real as the present, so that her husband's life was still 'there', though no longer accessible to her. The argument made in favour of the block universe runs as follows. If one observer sees two events as simultaneous, while another sees them as occurring at different times, does this not show that time differences are not fundamentally significant, even illusory, and so there is no ontological difference between past, present, and future? Hence all three domains must be equally existent! However, the argument does not work. The property of simultaneity that is being appealed to simply corresponds to the way in which different observers organise their knowledge of the past. No observer has knowledge of a distant event until it is within that observer's past lightcone (he has to be able to have received a message about its occurrence). The event is then unambiguously past. The fact that different observers offer different schemes of description of the past cannot be used to establish the necessary reality of an 'already' existing future.

Another argument sometimes produced in favour of the block universe is that the equations of physics do not contain a representation of the present moment. (There is nothing special about $t = 0$, so to speak.) While this is true, only an extreme physicalist, supposing that physics is all, could use this as a reason for denying so basic a human experience as the passage of time. If physics cannot represent the present moment, so much the worse for physics.

The fact of the matter is that scientific considerations alone cannot decide between the block universe on the one hand, and an unfolding universe in which there is a moving present moment on the other. The question of which to choose is intrinsically metascientific, confirming the point stated earlier that the nature of temporality is ultimately a question for metaphysics rather than physics. It is certainly the case that special relativity does not define a cosmic present moment, but neither does it forbid its existence, provided it is hidden and undiscoverable from the point of view of local physics. In other words, provided that the experiments of terrestrial physics do not suffice to identify in a unique way the particular time axis involved in the definition of the moving present, there is no contradiction with experiment. For example, in an unfolding universe the body processes of the travelling twin and the stationary twin would have to be different, precisely in the way that special relativity requires, and this would simply induce in the twins different perceptions of the rate at which they are moving into the future. Putting the matter more technically, a cosmic time axis aligned with the present moment would define three-dimensional domains of cosmic simultaneity, but provided the laws of physics were such that the resulting structure of space-time was in accord with special relativity (invariant under Lorentz transformations, the physicists would say), there would be no conflict with experiment. In fact, in our particular universe, which on the largest scales is homogeneous, there is a natural choice of cosmic time, corresponding to that which the cosmologists use when they say that the age of the universe is 13.7 billion years.[7] Thus it is clear that science itself does not unambiguously endorse either the idea of the block universe or the idea of an unfolding cosmic time. The choice between them requires metaphysical argument, in which theological considerations can quite properly play a role.[8] Physics constrains metaphysics, but it no more determines it than the foundations of a house determine the precise form of the building erected on them.

The block universe corresponds to the way in which the concept of divine knowledge of the created world was classically expressed in the writings of Boethius, Augustine, and Aquinas. They understood God to be wholly outside of time, looking down from eternity, so to speak, onto the whole of created history, with the space-time continuum laid out before the divine gaze *totum simul*, all at once. In other words, what God sees is indeed the block universe. Theologically, one must surely believe that God knows all things absolutely truthfully, that is to say, in full accord with their actual natures. This would then seem to imply that classical theology implicitly endorsed the metaphysics of the block universe, though this claim is seldom, if ever, explicitly made in the theological literature.

On the other hand, if the unfolding universe is the right metaphysical picture, then the truthful character of divine knowledge will surely imply that God knows that world according to its developing nature. In other words, God will not simply know that events are successive (occurring in the before/after ordering corresponding to the lightcone structure of space-time), but God will know them in their succession (the becoming of the present that continuously turns future potentiality into past actuality). This would require the divine acceptance of a genuine experience of temporality, a concept that corresponds to what has come to be called by some 'open theology.'[9] The question of what time is God's time is not as perplexing as one might at first suppose. The likeliest answer would seem to be that time, already mentioned, which the cosmologists use in their accounts of cosmic history. However, whatever is the true divine time axis, problems of simultaneity do not arise for God, since for the omnipresent divine Observer there is no such thing as a distant event. The Creator will know every event of creation exactly as and when it happens.[10]

A number of comments may be made about open theology's revision of the thinking of classical theology. No one who takes this point of view wishes to deny that there is a steadfast and unchanging dimension to divinity. The idea of divine eternity is not abandoned, but it is held in a complementary relationship with divine temporality. Thus what is being proposed is a dipolar, eternal/temporal, concept of deity. Process theology drew just such a notion from its appeal to the metaphysical thinking of Alfred North Whitehead.[11] However, Whitehead's scheme makes the eternal pole (the divine 'primordial nature') and the temporal pole (the divine 'consequent nature') matters of metaphysical necessity, imposed upon deity. A more orthodox open theology sees, on the contrary, God's acceptance of an engagement with time as an act of divine condescension by the Creator, who is graciously willing to share in the unfolding history of creation. According to this view, the divine polarity originates within the life and will of God and it is not imposed upon it from without by some over-riding metaphysical principle. It is part of the Creator's decision to bring into being a temporal world.

Open theology can be seen as part of a broad strand of theological thinking that has been particularly influential in recent years. Its central concept is an understanding that the act of creation involves a kenosis, or self-limitation, on the part of the Creator who, out of love for creation, freely suspends part of the exercise of absolute divine prerogatives.[12] At least three kinds of kenosis can be considered as being involved. First, God's absolute eternity is qualified by the acceptance of a complementary temporality, in the way that we have been discussing. Second, God's almighty power is qualified as creatures are allowed to be themselves and, through evolutionary processes, to make themselves. (This will be discussed further in chapter 5.) Classical theology pictured God as the cause of all things through the working of a primary causality, mysteriously active in and under the apparent secondary causalities exercised by creatures. As a result, the history of the world came to be thought of as resembling the performance of a predestined score written in eternity. Open theology pictures God as in providential interaction with divinely ordained natural processes and with the divinely allowed acts of free agents. On this view, the history of the universe is understood to resemble an unfolding improvisation in which the Creator is ceaselessly at work to bring about a harmonious resolution of the great multi-part fugue of creation. Third, God's omniscience can be understood to be qualified by the acceptance of temporality, so that it is seen as being a current omniscience (knowing all that it is possible to know now), rather than an absolute omniscience (knowing all that it will ever be possible to know). This is no divine imperfection, since in an unfolding world of true becoming the future is not yet there to be known. This third aspect of creatorly kenosis is particularly contentious, but it seems to be a necesssary consequence of a genuine divine engagement with time.[13]

A dipolar theology can appeal to scripture in support of its picture of divine temporality. The idea of the God of steadfast love who continually engages with the unfolding contingencies of history is very much in accord with the way that the Bible portrays God's relationship with Israel, even to the anthropomorphic point of saying that God changes God's mind as circumstances alter. It is also evidently consonant with Christian belief in the incarnation, the doctrine of the Word made flesh in a human life lived at a particular period of history and in a particular place. We may note also that the scientist-theologians who seek to do theology in the context of science have shown a clear inclination to taking a dipolar view of deity.[14]

The logical independence of issues of causality from issues of temporality means that no deductive link can be made between the block universe or an unfolding universe on the one hand, and determinism or indeterminism on the other. We noted earlier that issues of temporality concern the nature of time in itself, while causal issues relate to the kind of relationships existing between the events located in space and time. Aquinas emphasised that his 'block-universe' understanding of divine knowledge was perfectly compatible with the exercise of free choice by human agents. While divine foreknowledge might seem to threaten that freedom (though later the Jesuit Luis de Molina attempted ingeniously, but to my mind unsuccessfully, to suggest the contrary with his concept of 'middle knowledge'), for the God who perceives the whole of history *totum simul* there is no such foreknowledge, since all events are equally contemporaneous to the atemporal divine gaze. Another illustration of the independence of causal and temporal schemas is provided by the fact that the strictly deterministic world view propounded by Pierre Simon Laplace on the basis of his interpretation of Newtonian physics, in which total knowledge of the present implied complete retrodictive/predictive knowledge of both past and future, was nevertheless one that accommodated the idea of an unfolding absolute time in the Newtonian manner.

One further temporal topic deserves attention. Both in the external observations of the scientists (the apparent traces of past events) and in the internal experiences of all human beings (memories), there seems to be a directionality present in time, distinguishing past from future. This perception is often expressed in terms of the image of the arrow of time. In fact, at least four such arrows can be discerned. One is the arrow of cosmic history, pointing in the direction of the universe's expansion from the big bang. A second is the thermodynamic arrow, pointing in the direction of increasing entropy (disorder) in isolated systems. A third is the organisational arrow, pointing in the direction of the emergence of subsystems of increasing complexity, and most strikingly illustrated by the terrestrial phenomena of the development of life and conscious beings. The fourth is the psychological arrow, pointing from a past that we can remember towards a future that we do not yet know. The four arrows are logically distinct in their natures, but they all point in the same direction. Why there is this coincidence is not fully understood, but a number of points can be made.

Superficially there might seem to be a contradiction between the second and third arrows, the pessimistic arrow of increasing disorder and the optimistic arrow of increasingly highly complex systems, but this is not the case. Entropy certainly increases for isolated systems – this is the statement of the celebrated second law of thermodynamics – but those complex systems, such as living beings, which emerge and maintain themselves are not isolated. They are what scientists call dissipative systems, in continuous energetic interaction with their environment, exporting entropy and sustaining order, so that they can maintain their internal organisation. This is why animals have to eat and excrete. Every time we breathe out carbon dioxide, we expel entropy.

The second law of thermodynamics is particularly interesting since it differs in its character from the other fundamental laws of nature. The basic constituent laws of nature, with one small exception that is genuinely unimportant for the present discussion, are time-reversible. To understand what this means, consider the imaginative notion of a 'film' made of two electrons interacting. (Of course,

Heisenberg's uncertainty principle would not permit such a 'film' to have much clarity, but the idea is being used as a schematic device to convey a point whose exact expression would require a greater degree of mathematical sophistication than is being assumed in this book.) Time reversibility means that the 'film' would make equal physical sense whether it was run forwards or backwards. In other words, in the realm of fundamental micro-physics there is no intrinsic arrow of time. Yet, in the world of macro-physics, there certainly is such an arrow. A film in which shattered pieces of glass come together to form a perfect goblet is definitely being run backwards. In the everyday world we see transitions from order (goblet) to disorder (broken glass), but never vice versa. The latter transitions are not absolutely forbidden by the laws of physics, but they are infinitely unlikely, because they would require highly special, precisely correlated, initial conditions, perfect to a degree of exactitude that in practice is unattainable. Effectively, therefore, entropy increases in the macroscopic world, thus defining an irreversible direction of time because, in the absence of external intervention, disorder is overwhelmingly more probable than the kind of exquisite finely tuned orderliness that would enable the shattered glass to reassemble. The second law of thermodynamics is a statistical law, stating what is virtually bound to happen, not an absolute law stating what inexorably must always happen. The property of time-irreversibility appears to emerge from a time-reversible substrate when systems become so complicated that they cannot be described in constituent detail, and the multitude of their future options is so great that the most probable overall outcome, averaged over unknown constituent details, comes to dominate over the particularity of the merely possible. The accumulation of past memories is also an irreversible process, with a clear before and after, and it seems quite reasonable to suppose that here there may be some clue to the alignment of the psychological and thermodynamic arrows.

Judaism, Christianity, and Islam all have a strongly linear picture of time, which they see as a pilgrim path to be trodden. They are naturally comfortable with the concept of time's multiple and aligned arrows. The Eastern religions take a more cyclic view of time, viewing it as the circling revolutions of a samsaric wheel. In this particular respect, it is possible that they may find themselves less comfortable than the Abrahamic faiths when seeking understanding in the context of science.

4

Persons and value

———◆◆◆———

Blaise Pascal, though confessing himself daunted by the evidence beginning to emerge in the course of the seventeenth century of the immensity of the universe, nevertheless affirmed that human beings are greater than all the stars, since we know them and ourselves, and they know nothing. The coming into being of the self-conscious genus homo was an astonishing development in cosmic history. Thereby the universe became aware of itself and, as a by-product, science became an eventual possibility. After almost fourteen billion years, the universe was a world with persons in it.

Science prides itself on its concentration on what is objectively accessible, leading to conclusions that can readily be intersubjectively agreed. Its great secret weapon is experiment, the recourse to investigations that, at least in principle and quite often in practice, can be repeated at will by those who might doubt the testimony of others. Experiments have this quality of repeatability because they operate as probes of those aspects of reality that can be stripped down to the commonly accessible level of bare impersonality. Anything specifically idiosyncratic is bracketed out of consideration. The individualities of the experimenters – their past experiences and their present preferences – are of no formal relevance to the act of empirical enquiry. As a methodological strategy, this approach has proved brilliantly effective, and it has been responsible for much of the remarkable success achieved by science. A narrow focus has enabled a great deal of detail to be seen with considerable clarity. Yet much also lies outside of science's chosen field of view. As a metaphysical strategy for the formation of a total world view, scientific concentration on objective and impersonal data alone would be woefully inadequate. To suppose the contrary is to commit the error of scientism, the rash and implausible claim that science tells us all that is worth knowing, or even that could ever be known. Embracing that belief is to take an arid and dreary view of reality, to see the world as a kind of lunar landscape, devoid of persons and populated only by metastable, replicating and information-processing systems. Reductive physicalists are, of course, persons too, and so there seems to be an inherent contradiction between their official position and their actual experience. They have driven themselves to proclaim that almost all that makes life most valuable is actually epiphenomenal, a merely personal froth on the surface of an impersonal reality.[1] To impose the methodological context of science upon the ontological scope of human thinking would be to disable thought about a world that is too rich in its nature to be contained within such a reductionist straightjacket.

It is possible to illustrate the inadequacy of scientism from within the actual experience and practice of doing science itself. The search for an understanding as complete as possible, if pursued scrupulously, cannot be contained within the narrow bounds of scientific analysis, for the degree of science's epistemic success points us beyond the explanatory domain of science itself. It turns out that the context within which the human experience of science can be fully understood must exceed the merely scientific.

That human beings are able, in the course of their daily encounters, to gain a good understanding of everyday events is scarcely surprising. The evolutionary necessity to survive doubtless offers an explanation. It has become popular to appeal to the power of evolutionary influences in shaping the development of brains capable of coping with everyday experiences, and then to go on to treat this insight as if it were the clue to explaining human epistemic abilities in general.[2] I do not question that a degree of truth is contained in the arguments of evolutionary epistemology as far as certain human powers of mundane understanding are concerned. Nevertheless, such appeals are not sufficient by themselves to explain the extraordinary range of science's success. This deficit remains the case even when the need for survival is supplemented by arguments based on the effects of sexual selection. They involve appealing to the evolutionarily effective power that is associated with characteristics that are capable of attracting the attentions of the opposite sex, resulting in a consequent enhanced success in genetic propagation, a phenomenon that is strikingly exemplified by the peacock's tail. Flattering though it might be to suppose that the rational gifts necessary for scientific investigation will have proved in the course of hominid evolution to be irresistibly attractive to prospective mates, and so evolutionarily favoured, it scarcely seems a plausible notion to entertain.

The fact is that the universe has proved to be astonishingly transparent to scientific enquiry, resulting in an achievement too profound for evolutionary argument to be able to afford an adequate explanation. Human beings understand the subatomic world of quantum physics, and the cosmic realm of curved space-time, at least as well as the middle-scale world of the everyday. Yet these domains of the very small and the very large are not only remote from direct impact on human experience and survival, but they also require for their understanding counterintuitive modes of thought, quite different from those that have been developed to cope with mundane circumstances. Quantum theory's superposition principle is a case in point. To regard these esoteric successes as simply fortuitous spin-offs from evolutionary necessity is to make an unwarranted and implausible conjecture. From its own resources, science is unable to offer an adequate explanation of its impressive success.

Putting the matter more directly, science cannot validate its own basic premise, the indispensable act of faith that underlies all of its activity. Fundamental to the scientific enterprise is belief in the possibility of access to the basic structure of an intelligible universe. From a scientistic point of view, the possibility of deep science can only be regarded as resting on the incredibly happy accident that the universe has been found to have this fortunate character of rational transparency, and that we have proved to be persons capable of exploiting the opportunity that this affords. Strangest of all, it has turned out that the key to unlocking these deep secrets is provided by the abstract subject of mathematics. It is an actual technique of discovery in fundamental physics to seek theories whose mathematical formulation is in terms of what mathematicians recognise as being beautiful equations. (Mathematical beauty is related to qualities such as economy and elegance, together with the fact that profound consequences are found to stem from seemingly simple origins, a property the mathematicians call being 'deep'.) The universe is not only rationally transparent to us, but it is also rationally beautiful, rewarding those who investigate it with the experience of wonder at what is disclosed to their enquiry.

Those who reflect on these facts of profound cosmic intelligibility will surely want to attain an understanding of their source, and this must be sought from outside of science itself. Einstein once said that the only incomprehensible thing about the universe is that it is comprehensible. Yet, what for the scientist, as a scientist, is simply the miraculous fact that the physical world is deeply and wonderfully intelligible, can become in its turn comprehensible in the light of theological understanding, since belief in God enables one to see cosmic intelligibility and the beautiful ordering of the universe as reflections of the rational character of the world's Creator. I believe that scientists' almost instinctive recourse to 'Mind of God' language in their more popular writings bears testimony to the power of this idea, even if it is often only unconsciously entertained. Human access to the beautiful patterns of fundamental physics can be understood as an aspect of that ancient and powerful truth that we are persons 'made in the image of God' (Genesis 1:26).

There is a second way in which the actual practice of a conventionally impersonal science points one towards the acknowledgement of a significance beyond its self-chosen confines. This lies in a fact about scientific method to which brief reference has already been made in earlier chapters. Michael Polanyi used his own experience of scientific research to emphasise that it requires the exercise of tacit personal skills of judgement, such as those that experimentalists require when they seek to eliminate spurious 'background' effects that might otherwise contaminate their results, and those that theorists require when they select theoretical options on the basis not only of narrow empirical adequacy, but also on grounds of economy, comprehensiveness, and naturalness of argument, characteristics which have time and again proved reliable guides to long-term theoretical fruitfulness.[3] (The physicists' search for beautiful equations is a particular example of the exercise of this latter skill.) Such abilities do not come simply from book-study, but they have to be learnt through apprenticeship to the practice of a truth-seeking community. They involve the exercise of tacit skills that cannot be reduced to following the instructions of a written protocol. These acts of scientific judgement could not be incorporated into a computer programme, for they are intrinsically the activities of persons. That is why Polanyi called his book about the nature and practice of science, *Personal Knowledge*.

Yet, although the nature of personhood is a metascientific issue, our understanding of it will be influenced, even if not determined, by scientific insights. Human persons are embodied and the context of science strongly encourages taking a psychosomatic view of human nature in preference to some form of a Cartesian dualism of soul and body. (Since the predominant biblical view is that men and women are animated bodies rather than incarnated souls, this should not cause a problem for theology, despite its frequent historical tendency to incline to platonism.) The evolutionary kinship of homo sapiens with other animals points in the psychosomatic direction. Furthermore, the effects of drugs and brain damage on human personality are only too apparent, and they too encourage a psychosomatic stance. Contemporary neuroscience increasingly indicates a close connection between mental experience and the state of the brain. Its investigations are to be welcomed, yet their interpretation needs to be careful and judicious. The detailed light that at present they can throw onto the nature of personhood is very limited. That certain specific areas of the brain are found to be activated in the course of religious meditation is interesting, but only what one would expect in persons who are truly embodied beings. No doubt other specific areas of the brain are activated in the course of scientific thinking. These facts do not of themselves establish anything about the nature of the reality being encountered through such psychosomatic processes, whether scientific or religious. They do not justify a reductionist claim that the activity of religion – or science – amounts to no more than the occurrence of certain neural processes, or that thought can be strictly identified with patterns of synaptic firing, rather than its simply being correlated with them.

In other words, all the evidence for the connection between mind and brain can be taken absolutely seriously without inferring the identification of the mental as a mere epiphenomenon of the material. The fact that all our knowledge of the material world comes to us through mental activity helps to make the stance of reductive physicalism highly unpersuasive. Instead one should seek a more nuanced account that takes the mental and the material with equal seriousness, picturing them as united in a complementary relationship of psychosomatic unity. The task of finding such an account, often called dual-aspect monism,[4] is a formidable one, as surely must be the case for any adequate attempt to understand the subtle complexity of human personhood. Nevertheless, a number of contemporary scientific insights provide some modest but helpful clues.

Science is just beginning to be able to study the detailed behaviour of complex systems. Previously, its principal technique had been methodological reductionism, based on the decomposition of complex systems into their simpler constituent elements. When it came to large composite systems themselves, the best that had seemed available was the thermodynamic strategy of averaging over the hidden details of a great multitude of constituent properties, in order to produce a coarse-grained account of bulk properties, such as the temperature, pressure, and density of a gas. Today, the infant science of complexity theory is attempting to do something more ambitious. So far, the systems it has been able to study are only modestly complex, far simpler than even a single living cell. Much of the work is based on studying the detailed behaviour of computerised models possessing a manageable degree of complex structure. The present character of the subject is that of natural history rather than mature science, since it works with what is found to happen in particular instances, rather than being able to develop general theories of what makes it happen. Nevertheless, even at this preliminary level of investigation, some remarkably intriguing and unexpected properties have come to light. Some of the flavour of the subject can be given by describing a particular model studied by Stuart Kauffman, one of the pioneers in this new field.[5]

The system he considers is a logical structure, which means that it can readily be emulated on a computer. Technically, the system is a Boolean net of connectivity two, but its character is more accessibly conveyed in terms of an equivalent hardware model. This would be constituted by a large array of electric light bulbs, each of which can be in one of two states, 'on' or 'off'. The system develops in steps, according to some simple rules whose detailed nature need not concern us here. Each bulb is correlated with two other bulbs somewhere else in the array and the rules specify precisely how the next state of that bulb is determined by the present states of its two correlates. The system is started off in a random pattern of illumination and then left to develop according to this scheme. One might have supposed that nothing very interesting would happen and that the system would just twinkle away haphazardly for as long as it was allowed to do so. This is far from being the case. Very soon a remarkable degree of orderly behaviour sets in and the system cycles through only a very limited number of patterns of illumination. If there are ten thousand bulbs in the array, it turns out that there will only be about one hundred of these different patterns of illumination. Since for this system there are 2^{10000}, or about 10^{3000}, different possible states of illumination, this represents the spontaneous generation of an absolutely astonishing degree of order. (More generally, an array with N bulbs will cycle through about $N^{1/2}$ patterns.) Such remarkable behaviour is absolutely unforeseeable in terms of studying the individual relationships defining the array.

This capacity of complex systems spontaneously to generate remarkable patterns of ordered behaviour is not confined to logical models. It is also encountered in physical dissipative systems, held far from equilibrium by the exchange of energy and entropy with their environment.[6] A simple example is Bénard convection. Fluid is contained between two horizontal plates, the lower of which is heated in order to maintain a temperature difference with the upper plate. In certain well-defined circumstances, the convective motion of the hot fluid forms a regular pattern of hexagonal convection cells. This involves the self-organised correlation of the motions of trillions upon trillions of molecules.

So what is happening? At present we do not know. There must surely be some profound theory that lies behind the spontaneous self-organising powers of complex systems, but what that theory is has not yet been discovered. However, we can make some conjectures about the general shape that such a theory might be likely to take.

The self-organising behaviour, found in systems either logical or physical in character and relating to the pattern of their behaviour taken as a whole, strongly suggests that science's traditional reductionist laws, assigning prime significance to the exchange of energy between constituents, will need eventually to be supplemented by holistic laws concerned with the structured behaviour of systems considered in their totalities, for which the key concept will not be energy itself but something one might call 'information', the specification of dynamical patterns of behaviour and energy flow. This informational concept is not yet fully and sharply defined, but these are early days.[7] One might recall how long it took nineteenth-century physicists to sort out properly the concept of the conservation of energy. I am bold enough to conjecture that by the end of the twenty-first century, an appropriately formulated concept of information will have taken its place alongside energy as a fundamental category in science.

These developments, actual and anticipated, provide a scientific context that offers the prospect of at least the glimmer of an understanding of how to begin to think about the psychosomatic nature of persons. The complementarities of constituent/holistic and energy/information bear some modest degree of analogy with the much more profound and challenging complementarities of material/mental and brain/mind. In chapter 7 we shall explore how one might use these ideas to reconceptualise the idea of the human soul. All this seems promising, but further discussion is needed if one is to explore the matter with the carefulness it demands.

Although Kauffman's model is very interesting, its character as a logical system implemented on a computer means that the remarkable emergence of holistic order that it manifests arises in a completely deterministic way solely from the behaviour of its constituent elements. In other words, the model is intrinsically reductionist in causal structure, despite the holistic behaviour that it generates. The flow of causal ordering within it must be wholly from bottom (constituents) to top (totality). There is no opposite top-down causality actually operating as an independent causal principle by which the whole genuinely influences in an independent way the behaviour of the parts.

This fact implies a significant disanalogy with the sought-for understanding of embodied persons, considered as being capable of acting as agents precisely through the top-down influence of mental decisions on physical actions. Without this power of agency, human beings would be no more than immensely elaborate automata. If that were so, not only would claims of true freedom of action as responsible moral agents be subverted, but also the claims of truly rational discourse, since human utterances would be seen to be no more than automatic mouthings. I believe that human freedom is basic to our character as rational and responsible beings. It is a fundamental characteristic of personhood. Of course, I know that some philosophers question this, believing that a compatibilist understanding that links thoughts, desires, and actions in a single grand deterministic nexus is sufficient. Yet the mere conjunction of action and an only seemingly selective choice is surely not enough for real freedom of agency. A robot could be programmed to go through a doorway while at the same time uttering the words 'I want to go through here', but it would just be an automaton all the same. My rejection of the compatibilist view is made easier by the recognition that it is by no means a necessary deduction from what we can actually learn from modern science. We shall see that physical systems differ from logical systems in being open to the possibility of the operation of top-down causal influence.

The fact is that important scientific discoveries of the twentieth century have given us the possibility of a picture of the processes of the universe that is capable of accommodating human freedom. We have noted already that the world of mere mechanism, which seemed to many in the eighteenth century to be the implication of Newtonian physics, has broken down to yield something much more interesting. Widespread intrinsic unpredictabilities have been found in physical processes, both at the level of microscopic events (quantum theory) and at the level of macroscopic events (chaos theory's account of many systems with an extreme sensitivity to external influences, however small the latter may be). It is important to be clear about the intrinsic character of these unpredictabilities. They are matters of principle, and not matters of current deficiencies of investigative practice. It is not possible that the development of more exact forms of measurement, or of more precise forms of calculation, would be able to remove them. The existence of these intrinsic unpredictabilities shows that the physical world is not a clockwork universe of mere mechanism, but something altogether more subtle than that. It is a metaphysical option to believe that it is also more supple.

Unpredictability is an epistemological property, concerned with what we can or cannot know. There is no logically inevitable connection between epistemology on the one hand, and ontology's account of what is actually the case on the other hand. Whatever connection is made is a matter for metaphysical decision. Immanuel Kant notoriously disconnected the two, alleging that human beings can only know phenomena (the appearances of things) and not noumena (things in themselves). Scientists, on the other hand, take a wholly different tack. The philosophical context of scientific practice is a commitment to realism, the belief that what we know is a reliable guide to what is actually the case. Without the conviction that science's knowledge is actually telling us what the physical world is like, it is difficult to see why the labour and not infrequent frustration involved in pure scientific research should ultimately be considered worthwhile. This conviction is reinforced by the way in which the physical world so frequently proves radically different from our prior expectation (think, once more, of quantum theory). The feel of doing science is the feel of discovery. It is the nudge of nature that shapes our scientific thinking.

To the thorough-going realist, for whom epistemology is the reliable guide to ontology, intrinsic unpredictabilities will not just be unfortunate patches of unavoidable ignorance (epistemological deficits), but they will be seen as signs of some form of openness in physical process (ontological opportunities). In the case of quantum theory, this approach has been the one almost universally adopted. Almost all physicists interpret Heisenberg's uncertainty principle (discovered as an epistemic limitation on what can be measured) as an actual ontological principle of indeterminacy. This is despite the fact that there is an alternative interpretation of quantum theory, due to David Bohm, which entails the same experimental consequences as the conventional interpretation, but has them arising from a basic scheme that is deterministic, but with only a partial possibility of observational access to a knowledge of the causal factors at work.[8] For Bohm, Heisenberg's uncertainty principle is simply a matter of necessary ignorance. Here we see clearly how physics on its own is not sufficient to settle the metaphysical issue of the nature of causality. The choice between Bohr and Bohm has to be made on other grounds than that of empirical adequacy. Those physicists who reflect on their preference for Bohr over Bohm will attribute it to metascientific factors, such as the perception of an unforced naturalness in the Copenhagen approach, compared with what seems an unattractive air of contrivance in Bohm's ingenious theory.

In the case of chaotic unpredictabilities, this realist strategy has been less popular. However, I have espoused it, pointing out that the Newtonian equations from which the recognition of chaos first arose, and which have led many to talk solely of in terms of 'deterministic chaos', are in any case known to be no more than approximations to physical reality.[9] Therefore the deterministic character of these equations should not be made an illegitimate excuse for closing off other metaphysical options. Instead, the equations can be understood as being no more than what one might call 'downward emergent' approximations to the behaviour of a more supple reality. By downward emergent I mean the behaviour manifested in those special situations where a constituent picture, based on the possibility of separation of the system into smaller parts, together with the possibility of isolating and controlling environmental influences, is actually an acceptable approximation to what is happening. On this view of classical physics, its effectiveness arises simply from the fact that it is capable of giving a pragmatically successful account of large systems in those particular situations where such a high degree of separability is a feasible attainment. Exactly the same kind of separability is an indispensable condition for the possibility of experimental attempts to confirm the near-validity of the Newtonian equations held to apply to the system, for without it there would be such a degree of interconnection with the whole environment that one could not understand any particular thing without having had to understand everything else as well. These conditions of separability are far from being satisfied universally. For example, the extreme sensitivity of chaotic systems to the least perturbation arising from their environment means that generally they do not fulfil the condition. In other words, scientists only have feasible experimental access to a limited sample of actual occurrences. The apparent certainties of classical physics applied to macroscopic phenomena are open to revised assessment in more general circumstances.[10]

One might have supposed that the discussion could be carried further by a judicious combination of quantum and classical ideas, since the great sensitivity of chaotic systems means that their future behaviour soon comes to depend upon microscopic details to which Heisenberg forbids access. However, this blending of the two kinds of physics cannot be achieved in any straightforward way. This is because quantum theory has an intrinsic scale, set by Planck's constant, but the fractal character of chaotic behaviour (it looks the same on every scale) means that the two theories are incompatible, posing an unresolved problem for physics. This observation also illustrates the fact that physics' account of causal structure is distinctly patchy, good in certain domains, but lacking adequate understanding of how different domains relate to each other.[11]

Taking an open interpretation of unpredictabilities does not imply that the future is some form of random lottery. Rather, it is to allow the metaphysical possibility that there are further causal principles at work in bringing about that future beyond those that are described by science's bottom-up notion of the exchange of energy between constituents. An obvious candidate for such a principle, in view of what we know about the self-organising behaviour of dissipative systems, would be the top-down action of the whole upon the parts, of a pattern-forming kind. One might call such a principle 'active information'. Its existence would mark a significant difference between the metaphysical status of physical systems, on this view capable of possessing a genuine diversity of causal principles bringing about their future behaviour, and logical models of the Kauffman type, which we have already seen actually possess only bottom-up causality. Here would be a glimmer – one could not claim more than that – of how, in a highly generalised and vastly more complex situation, the acts of embodied agents might take place. When I decide to raise my arm, there are certainly bottom-up causes at work, such as the flow of currents in nerves and the contractions of muscles, but it is I, the total person, who am the agent executing the decision.

We certainly do not possess an adequate account of agency, despite our fundamental experience of it, but even so partial and tentative an approach as that sketched here is sufficient to defeat the defeaters, who wrongly say that science altogether forbids the concept of human free action. The truth is that taking seriously the context of science imposes no such demand. Physics has not established the causal closure of the world on its own restricted terms. I have also suggested that it might be through some analogous process of the input of pure information into open systems that divine providential interaction with history is exercised within the open grain of created nature – another phenomenon of which many religious believers would claim experience.[12] There will be further discussion of that issue in the chapter that follows. At this stage, let me remark that it is important to recognise that, without some such discussion as the foregoing, the concept of top-down causality is by no means an unproblematic notion to entertain, despite the fact that many theological writers seem simply to assume that this is so. Causality is surely a zero-sum game, so that some analysis of the kind attempted above, showing that bottom-up processes do not soak up all the available room for causal manoeuvre, is absolutely essential if there is to be a credible appeal to a role for top-down effects.

If these ideas have validity, it is clear that their extension to persons would require that the concept of information – acknowledged as not yet being clearly and fully formulated even in the case of the logical and physical systems discussed above – must receive further and much greater elaboration. Persons are certainly more than computers made of meat.[13] There is a great deal more to the nature of the mental pole of psychosomatic beings than can be represented simply in terms of patterns of dynamical behaviour or computational procedures. Computers are excellent at syntax, but they have no access to semantics. Yet encounter with meaning is central to human experience. Great conceptual enrichment would be necessary in the idea of 'information' if it were to begin to be able to accommodate the multiply complex character of personal experience, in contrast to the comparative impersonal simplicity of the kind of experience that science considers. Three matters are of particular significance and importance in the realm of the personal. One is an adequate account of the context within which personal beings have evolved and are able to operate. A second matter is the issue of consciousness, and the third is the issue of human perceptions of value.

The question of evolutionary context can be illustrated by considering human powers of mathematical reasoning and exploration. If the environment in which hominid evolution took place had been solely the physico-biological setting that conventional Darwinian thinking assumes, the only kind of mathematical skills that would have been expected to evolve would have been those that convey obvious survival advantages, such as elementary arithmetic and basic Euclidean geometry. Whence then has come our ability to investigate the properties of non-commutative algebras and to prove Fermat's Last Theorem? It strains credulity to treat them as just happy accidental spin-offs from mundane survival necessity. I believe that the evolutionary acquisition of these high intellectual skills is only intelligible if one is willing to recognise the existence of a noetic dimension of reality, which contains the truths of mathematics and also forms part of the context of human development.[14] Many mathematicians affirm belief in the existence of such a realm of mathematical reality, believing that in their work they are engaged in discovery, and not in the mere invention of amusing intellectual puzzles.[15] In their view, Benoit Mandelbrot did not devise his celebrated fractal set; he found it. If that is the case, the resulting enhanced context of hominid life makes it possible to understand the development of sophisticated mathematical abilities as the result of a process continually growing in scope and effectiveness as persons were drawn into the exploration of the realm of mathematical truth, motivated in this development, once it had begun, by intellectual delight rather than by survival necessity. No doubt this exploratory process was enabled psychosomatically by the well-known developmental plasticity of the human brain, whose intricate web of neuronal connectivity is largely shaped by experience, rather than being predetermined genetically. The Lamarckian process of inter-generational cultural influence would then have driven the development of increasing mathematical ability.

Turning to the second issue, that of consciousness, one must readily acknowledge that neuroscience has been making very impressive progress in discovering some of the neural pathways by which our brains process the information that they receive from the environment. We have noted also that other studies have identified certain regions of the brain that are particularly activated during specific forms of mental activity, including religious meditation. These results are of great interest and one must hope for further progress in this kind of work. However, it is important to recognise that there is a deep chasm of ignorance yawning between neuro-scientific talk of this kind, undoubtedly valuable and interesting though it is, and the simplest conscious experiences, such as feeling a toothache or seeing red. The problem of qualia – how it is that 'feels' such as these arise – is very far from being solved, and the problem of understanding the source of our basic experience of being aware of ourselves is equally difficult. (It is far from evident that awareness, as opposed to information-processing, has an obvious survival value, for possessing a definite focus of attention might lead to the neglect of peripheral dangers.) Here we encounter the 'hard problem' of consciousness.[16] It cannot be finessed by Procrustean attempts to dismiss accounts of these mental experiences (which, in fact, we know as surely as we know anything) as being mere 'folk psychology', the kind of subjective knowledge which, it is claimed, a true scientist ought to be quite happy to disregard.[17] No person should be content to be so dismissive of basic personal experience.

Of course, I do not rejoice at our current ignorance in thinking about the nature of consciousness. But neither am I inclined to succumb to talk that suggests that consciousness is the 'last frontier', which the conquering armies of an heroic science are just about to cross. The problems are far too deep for that kind of facile triumphalist expectation. It is just conceivable that the problem of consciousness is one that will for ever lie beyond the impersonal grasp of science. Pretty much all else that scientists study, whether it concerns properties of matter or the processes of life, can be treated in a mode external to us as persons, and so it is available for a degree of impersonal experimental investigation. Consciousness is different, however, for it is essentially private and fundamental to our constitution as personal beings. I do not have direct access to any other person's consciousness, and when I think about my own consciousness, I cannot divorce that thought from whatever it is that I actually have in my mind's eye at that moment. This individual and reflexive nature of consciousness gives it a unique character, which might mean that human beings will never be able to attain a full understanding of its nature by means of purely scientific methods of enquiry. If that proves to be the case, it would by no means give grounds for denying the mysterious reality of our conscious experience. The very existence of the context of science depends upon the prior existence of human persons and it would be the height of folly to try to take a reductionist saw in order to sever the epistemic branch upon which we all have to sit.

The third issue, the significance of value, is of central importance in any attempt to frame an adequate metaphysics. Science is conventionally described as being value-free and there is an important sense in which this is clearly true. An overt appeal to value plays no formal role in the structure of scientific argument. The editors of the *Physical Review* would not accept a paper about quarks based on the claim that this is how they ought to behave. The only acceptable scientific argument appeals to the way in which quarks have actually been found to behave. Yet the practice of science itself is not value-free. Its truth-seeking activity depends upon the scientific community subscribing to the values of the accurate reporting of discoveries and the generous sharing of ideas. In addition, we have seen that appeals to certain values, such as elegance and economy, play a significant role in the search for theoretical understanding. They can function as guides to the formulation of ideas, as when Paul Dirac said that he made his great discoveries in quantum theory through a single-minded search for beautiful equations. In this case the discernment of these values is being employed as an heuristic strategy, but it is not in itself being presented as forming the basis of a justifying argument. Yet this search for beautiful equations is no act of aesthetic indulgence on the part of theoretical physicists, since three centuries of experience endorse it as a method for finding theories whose long-term fruitfulness is persuasive of their verisimilitudinous character. Dirac discovered a celebrated equation (inscribed on his memorial tablet in Westminster Abbey), which was found to combine quantum theory and special relativity in a wonderfully elegant manner. It was an entirely unexpected gift that the equation turned out also to predict the existence of antimatter, a previously unknown phenomenon. Such explanatory excess is highly persuasive that true insight has been gained into the actual character of nature.

Thus it has turned out, as we noted earlier, that the universe is not only rationally transparent to scientific enquiry, but it has also proved to be rationally beautiful, rewarding scientists with the experience of wonder at the marvellous order which is revealed through the labours of their research. From a strictly scientific point of view this is an unanticipated and unexplained bonus, additional to the gift of cosmic intelligibility itself. The deep order of the universe has been found to possess a highly significant character that surely needs to be treated as more than fortuitous.

Responding to the challenge to understand this has brought about a revival of natural theology, pursued in a revised form when compared with the old-style physico-theology of John Ray and William Paley. Paley had largely appealed to the marvellous aptness of living beings, claimed as constituting a sign that they were the products of a divine Designer. Charles Darwin undermined the force of this argument by showing how the evolutionary accumulation and sifting of small differences through the processes of natural selection taking place over the long periods of deep time could produce the appearance of design without calling for the direct intervention of a Designer. With hindsight one can see that the physico-theologians had made the mistake of invoking theological explanation where science was perfectly competent to do what is its proper task. The new natural theology does not attempt to rival science on its own explanatory ground, but rather it complements science by setting its discoveries in a more comprehensive context of understanding.

Its argument looks not to occurrences, such as the development of the eye, but to the laws of nature that underly the form and possibility of all occurrence, and which science has to treat simply as given brute facts. These laws, in their economy and rational beauty, have a character that seems to point the enquirer beyond what science by itself is capable of telling, making a materialist acceptance of them as unexplained brute facts an intellectually unsatisfying stance to take. In contrast, the new natural theology is able to offer a degree of explanatory insight whose scope must necessarily elude the self-limited power of science alone. For example, I have already claimed that the rational beauty of fundamental physics is made intelligible if it is understood as a pale but true reflection of the Mind of the universe's Creator. The idea of a cosmic Intelligence behind the wonderful order of the world has appealed not only to those who stand within a religious tradition,[18] but also to those who have no such traditional belief.[19] The picture of God offered by this new natural theology is not that of Paley's Ingenious Artificer, intervening in physical process, but the One who is the ground of the fruitful order that makes any process possible at all. There is no theological need to try to seek gaps in natural process, of the kind that the Intelligent Design movement has claimed to identify. Instead, the possibility of this new natural theology arises from the realisation that the context of science has a character that demands more explanation than science itself can provide, thereby affording theistic understanding the opportunity of offering additional fruitful insight.

One may summarise the argument by noting that within Western thought there have been two distinct kinds of metaphysical scheme, each offering an overarching view that claims to encompass adequately the whole human encounter with reality. The two schemes differ in what they take as the unexplained ground for their proffered explanations. No scheme can be formulated without some such a priori assumption, for nothing comes of nothing. The materialist scheme is based on the brute fact of the existence and properties of matter; the theistic scheme is based on the brute fact of the will of a divine creatorly Agent. The claim of the new natural theology is that the latter is to be preferred because materialism stops short of giving an account of the laws of nature that is adequate to their observed character, which is too remarkable to be treated as simply inexplicably given. Further argument to this effect will be given in the next chapter.

However, from a theological point of view this new kind of natural theology on its own yields only a thin conception of deity, not going beyond the idea of the Cosmic Architect or the Great Mathematician. This fact is scarcely surprising, since limited evidence can only lead to limited insight and this kind of natural theology only appeals to very general aspects of the human encounter with reality. Such a revised natural theology, with its emphasis on considerations such as the structure of the laws of nature, considers only a small fraction of the evidence to which a more developed theology can look for motivating its beliefs. Nevertheless, such limited insight should not be despised.

Looking beyond the narrow confines of science, we discern a world that is shot through with value to a quite extraordinary and significant degree. Ask a scientist, as a scientist, to tell you all that he or she can about music, and one will say that it is a neural response to the impact of sound waves on the eardrum. Of course, that is true, and in its own way worth knowing, but ask a scientist as a person to tell you all that he or she can about music and one will surely have much more to say about its mysterious power to communicate a timeless beauty and to evoke a range of feelings and desires. Science trawls experience with a coarse-grained net, and much that is of the greatest significance slips through its wide meshes.

How does it come about that a temporal sequence of wave-packets of sound can induce in us this timeless encounter with beauty which, I believe, we should treat with the utmost attention and seriousness? It would be intolerably crass to regard aesthetic experience as epiphenomenal froth and to treat delight in beauty as no more than a temporary shift in the chemical balance of certain neurotransmitters. Of course, for embodied beings such as ourselves, there must be a material complement to any form of mental experience, and it is good when science can tell us something about what this counterpart might be, but that is only one aspect, and a small one at that, of the story of the human encounter with value.

Science engages with issues of value in a different way when it comes up against ethical problems. Science itself gives us knowledge, and I believe that this is a gift unambiguously to be welcomed, since knowledge is surely always a better basis for responsible decision than ignorance would be. But technology then takes science's knowledge and turns it into power, the ability to get things done. This is a much more ambiguous gift, for not everything that can be done, should be done. In order to choose the good and refuse the bad, human beings need the further gift of ethical wisdom. Religious traditions are by no means the sole sources of moral insight, but their centuries-old experience of wrestling with ethical perplexities means that they have much to offer.

I believe that all human beings have a degree of moral knowledge that exceeds what science might be able to explain in terms of evolutionary strategies for survival and gene propagation. Notions of kin altruism (protecting and propagating the family gene pool) and reciprocal altruism (helping an associate in the expectation of an eventual return) are enlightening and no doubt express part of the truth. The same could be said of game-theoretic maximal strategies, such as tit-for-tat (respond to others as they do to you). However, these insights do nothing to explain the kind of radical altruism that impels someone to risk their own life in the attempt to rescue an unknown and unrelated person from drowning. Anthropological accounts of diverse societies help us to see how cultural effects can mould the shape of public morality, but I am unable to believe that my ethical convictions, for example that torturing children is wrong and that there is a duty of care to the weak, are just conventions of my society. They are facts about the ethical reality within which we function as morally responsible persons.

Many deep aspects of personal experience elude the impersonal grasp of science. A strategy of scientistic reduction will either trivialise them as epiphenomenal, or else be driven to regard as inexplicable a very great deal of what is most precious in human life. Theistic belief offers a way out of this impasse. Just as the rational transparency and wonderful order of the physical world become intelligible if they are seen as reflecting the Mind of the world's Creator, so human experiences of beauty can be understood as a sharing in the joy that God takes in creation, and our ethical intuitions can be seen as originating in intimations of the good and perfect divine will. Science offers an illuminating context within which much theological reflection can take place, but in its turn it needs to be considered in the wider and deeper context of intelligibility that a belief in God affords. This gives us the way to take our experience of being persons with the utmost adequacy and seriousness. The context of science in no way discourages this recognition of the significance of the personal.

5

Consonance: creation, providence, and relationality

A major thesis of this book is that when theology is practised in the context of science what is involved is more than just a wrestling with those identifiable concerns that are obvious points of contact between science and theology. Of course, questions of this particular kind are undoubtedly important, and they have been the subject of much discussion over centuries. Yet, so far in this book our concern has been with more general and less-focused issues, relating to matters such as the style of discourse and the particularities of intellectual perspective that are appropriate to the science–religion dialogue. These concerns structure the shape of a contextual theology, thus making it clear that what is involved in the interaction of science and theology is more than simply attention to a few specific problems. Nevertheless, it is now time to recognise that there are also specific areas of our engagement with reality to which both science and theology seek to contribute, and there needs to be discussion of the inter-relationship of what they have to say about these matters.

Before looking into detailed issues, we should note that the existence of a chapter of this kind explains the non-existence of a chapter which might well have been expected to have a place in a contextual theology, namely one with the heading 'God'. The bottom-up thinking of a scientific contextual theology implies that its approach to deity will not be through general metaphysical discussion of the concept and nature of divinity, but rather it will seek its theological motivation in the divine economy, those acts of creation and revelation which are the chosen means of divine disclosure. We have already begun such an approach in the last chapter by discussing a revised form of natural theology, interpreting the wonderful order of the world as a sign of a divine Mind behind creation, and looking to God as the source of the values which structure and enrich personal experience.

66

The specific issues with which this chapter is concerned aim to carry this approach further by seeking mutual consonance between particular scientific discoveries and insights on the one hand and particular theological understandings of God's nature and will on the other.

Science gives an account of the nature and history of the universe; theology asserts the universe to be God's creation. Science offers its understanding of the processes of the world; theology affirms its belief that God is providentially active within that world's history. These statements are not in immediate competition with each other, since they operate at different categorical levels. A simple way of putting the matter would be to say that science's concern is with process (how things happen), and theology's concern is with purpose and meaning (why things are happening). Therefore science and theology are not direct rivals, as they would be if they were proposing conflicting replies to exactly the same questions. (We have seen that to assume the contrary, by supposing that theology could supply answers to science's questions about such matters as the development of the eye, was the mistake made in the eighteenth century by the physico-theologians.) The true relationship between science and theology is therefore complementary, rather than competitive. Yet this certainly does not imply that the two disciplines have nothing specific to say to each other. A positive dialogue is necessary, not least because the way each subject answers its own questions must bear some fitting relationship to the answers offered by the other, if it is indeed the one world of reality that both are seeking to speak about. There will be no strict logical entailment between the two sets of answers, but there certainly needs to be a significant degree of consonance. How? and Why? are distinct questions, but the forms of their answering must fit compatibly together. The responses given must be congruent. If someone says that their purpose is to make a cup of tea, and the method that they intend to employ involves putting the kettle in the refrigerator, we are rightly suspicious of what we have been told.

A contextual theology engaging seriously with science will therefore have to pay detailed attention to the traditional issues of creation and providence, approached from the perspective of a quest for consonance between the insights of science and religion. This chapter will also consider a rather different area of consonance, associated with a paradigm change that has come about in the way that science understands its own context. The twentieth century saw increasing recognition that the character of the physical world is deeply relational. Mere atomism is not enough, even to understand subatomic physics. Here the theologians were centuries ahead of the scientists, since trinitarian theology had long affirmed that the essential nature of the world's Creator is constituted by the relational life of the three divine Persons, and one might expect that to be reflected, however palely, in the character of God's creation. We start, however, by turning first to the subject of the doctrine of creation itself.

Creation

Many scientists fail to appreciate what is the proper focus of the theological doctrine of creation. Its concern is not with temporal origin (who lit the blue touchpaper for the big bang?), but with ontological origin (why is there something rather than nothing?). Stephen Hawking did not understand this point when he made his celebrated but naive remark that if space-time in the neighbourhood of the big bang was 'rounded off' in a spatial kind of way so as to remove a single identifiable point of initiation, as his speculative quantum cosmology had suggested, then there would be nothing left for a Creator to do.[1] On the contrary, theology asserts that God is as much the Creator today as God was 13.7 billion years ago, since it believes that at all times the universe is held in being by faithful divine decree. It is the Creator who ordains the laws of quantum theory and general relativity, whose consequences Hawking was seeking to explore. It is God who 'breathes fire into the equations and makes a universe for them to describe'.[2]

But what evidence could there be to suggest that the ontological origin of the cosmos lies in the will of its divine Creator? Belief in the world as a creation cannot be expected to mean that the universe will be found to be full of items clearly stamped 'Made by God'. Neither can one perform the ultimate experiment of removing the Creator and seeing if the universe disappears. A much more subtle approach is required if theology is successfully to scan the scientific story in quest of consonance with its own belief in the world as a divine creation. What can legitimately be looked for are hints – not proofs – of the presence of a divine Mind behind the order of the cosmos and the presence of a divine Purpose behind its unfolding history. The claim being made would not be that the universe cannot at all be understood solely from a scientific perspective, for that is manifestly untrue, but that it cannot be fully understood without setting it in a theological context. The doctrine of creation can make intelligible what from a purely scientific point of view has to be treated as brute fact or happy accident. Theology's role is to complement the scientific account, without pretending to replace it. In the last chapter we saw an example of this happening, when it was suggested that the rational transparency and rational beauty that science has encountered in its exploration of nature – striking facts that give science its opportunities for discovery and scientists the reward of wonder for their labours – need not be treated as inexplicably fortunate features of the world, but they can be made intelligible by interpreting them as reflections of the Mind of the Creator.

A second hint, relating in this case to the question of whether there is any sign of a divine purpose at work, has been given by a remarkable set of scientific insights recognised in the last forty years and gathered together under the rubric of the anthropic principle.[3] Scientists have come to realise that for a universe to be capable of evolving carbon-based life it has to be a very specific kind of universe indeed. Its laws of nature (which, remember, are given brute facts as far as science is concerned) have to take particular forms, and the forces that they specify have to have specific intrinsic strengths lying within very narrow margins. Otherwise carbon-based life could never have been able to evolve anywhere, or at any time, in cosmic history.

Take for an example the origin of carbon itself, the element that is of central importance in the chemical structure of living beings because of the role it plays in forming the long chain molecules that are the biochemical basis of life. No carbon was made during the initial aftermath of the big bang and, in fact, there is only one place in the whole universe where carbon actually can be made, in the interior nuclear furnaces of the stars. (Every atom of carbon in every living being was once inside a star – we are creatures made of stardust.) The processes involved in the stellar production of carbon are very delicately balanced, and it turns out that their feasibility constrains the strengths of the nuclear forces of nature to lie within narrow limits. There are further narrowly constrained properties of these forces which are needed in order to enable the production of the many other chemical elements also necessary for life. If nuclear physics had been only a little bit different, there could have been no carbon-based life at all, ever.

To take another example, the physics of the early universe has to be such that it neither flies apart too fast, thereby quickly becoming too dilute for interesting processes to occur, nor rapidly collapses in upon itself again, thereby destroying any nascent structures in a premature big crunch. Once again, constraints on the form of the laws of physics are necessary in order to avoid these cosmic catastrophes. The necessary balance has most probably been brought about by physical law taking a specific form that induced in the very early universe a process called inflation, a kind of momentary boiling of space whose smoothing effect resulted in an extremely close relation between the tendencies of expansion and gravitational attraction, thereby avoiding either too rapid dilution or too rapid collapse.

To take a final example, dark energy, a recently observed property of space itself which is partly responsible for cosmic expansion, is found to take a value one hundred and twenty orders of magnitude (powers of ten) smaller than a reasonable expectation based on quantum theory would have suggested might be the case, thereby avoiding the explosive cosmic expansion that would otherwise have occurred.[4] And so one could go on. Not only are there many conditions requiring a fine-tuning of the laws of nature if carbon-based life is to be at all possible, but it is also remarkable that these many constraints are mutually compatible, thereby permitting the existence of the universe that we inhabit. It is abundantly clear that a life-generating universe is a very special kind of universe indeed.

All scientists agree that this is so. Where the argument begins is whether there is any kind of metascientific significance attaching to these discoveries. Scientists instinctively prefer the general to the particular and so there was considerable prior expectation that our cosmos would turn out to be no more than a typical specimen of what a universe might be like. It came therefore as something of an unwelcome shock to many to discover anthropic particularity. Moreover the fine-tuning involved is so exacting that it seems less than rational to treat it as being just a happy accident. Of course, if the laws of nature had not been such as to allow eventual human evolution, then we would not be here to puzzle over fine-tuning (just as if the fifty highly trained marksmen in the firing squad had not all missed, the prisoner would not have been alive to wonder at his good fortune), but when highly improbable things happen that seem to carry striking significance, the rational thing to do is to see if there might not be a deeper explanation than simply attributing them to luck (might it not have been the case that the marksmen were on the prisoner's side and missed by design?[5]).

A possible explanation of anthropic particularity can be offered by theology, for it asserts that the universe is indeed not 'any old world', but a creation which can be understood to have been endowed by its Creator with precisely those properties that have enabled it to have a fruitful history. Sensing this threat of theism, some scientists sought an alternative metascientific explanation of fine-tuning. They came up with the notion of a multiverse, a grossly extended form of naturalism that supposes our world to be no more than a single member of an immense portfolio of many different universes, each distinct and separate from the others and each with its own specific form of the laws of nature. If this vast and unobservable array were sufficiently big and varied, then it would perhaps be no great surprise if one of its component worlds just by chance happened to be fine-tuned to permit the possibility of carbon-based life.[6] Of course, that world would be our world, since we are carbon-based life. According to this view, there is no great significance attached to anthropic fruitfulness – it simply corresponds to a random winning ticket in a multiversial lottery.

Of course the mere assumption of a multiverse would really explain nothing without there being some kind of independent motivation for accepting so prodigal a proposal, since the significance of any specific cosmic property, however remarkable, could always be dismissed simply by supposing the universe carrying it to be part of an assumed, arbitrarily large, portfolio of different worlds. Ingenious but highly speculative and uncertain theories, appealing to notions of a not yet properly formulated quantum cosmology, have been supposed by some to suggest the possibility of proliferating worlds, but I believe the sober scientific judgement to be that there is no sufficiently well-established motivation for belief in the existence of any universe other than the one that we can actually observe. Anything that goes beyond that is not science but a metascientific speculation. The multiverse proposal is ontologically prodigal and it seems to serve only one explanatory purpose – to defuse the threat of theism. In contrast, metascientific belief in a divine Creator does a number of other explanatory pieces of work, such as making the deep order of the cosmos intelligible and pointing to the source of the widely testified human experience of encounter with the sacred. There is a cumulative case for belief in God and a created universe, which does not seem to have a parallel in the case of the multiverse

In evaluating the willingness of many scientists to countenance the idea of a multiverse, it is important to be aware that contemporary fundamental physics has shown itself to be strikingly hospitable to speculations going far beyond the empirically accessible. During my time in the subject, it was largely experimentally driven and theorists were led to conceive and exploit new ideas under the intellectually healthy pressure of empirical discovery. This process resulted in the late 1970s in the establishment of what is now called 'the Standard Model', a very successful account of the nature of matter based on the theory of quarks. Since those days, however, two things have happened. There has been a comparative dearth of new empirical data, due to the high cost of the necessary experimental facilities, and there has been a corresponding willingness on the part of theorists to rely on mathematically based speculations, purporting to refer to processes many orders of magnitude beyond those of which we have direct empirical knowledge. A great deal of this speculation has centred on superstring theories.[7] The idea is to investigate relativistic quantum theory when it is formulated, not in terms of pointlike entities, but in terms of higher-dimensional structures. Many people of brilliant ability have been involved in this work, and the richness of relativistic quantum theory is such that it is certainly sensible to explore all of its potentialties as fully as possible. It was also encouraging that string theories incorporated gravity in an unforced and apparently consistent way. Yet without the presence of experimental constraint, there is no guarantee that the results obtained will be of any relevance to the actual nature of the physical world. The lessons of history are discouraging to the hope that we can second-guess nature on a scale more than sixteen orders of magnitude beyond the realm of our actual experience of encounter with it.[8]

The hope behind this work was originally that there might emerge a string theory that was unique, or almost unique, with few if any arbitrary parameters. This would have corresponded to the attainment of the so-called 'Holy Grail' of a Grand Unified Theory, or 'Theory of Everything' as some have been bombastically inclined to term it. This hope has not been fulfilled. For technical reasons, connected with the fact that string theories can only consistently be formulated in ten or eleven dimensions of space-time, the extra dimensions of which then have to be 'rolled-up' spontaneously in some way so as to yield an acceptable account of our actually experienced four-dimensional space-time world, the range of different realistic consequences that might flow from the theory has turned out to be vast. Some estimates put the number of such different possible worlds as high as 10^{500}. It is symptomatic of the speculative spirit of contemporary fundamental physics, that some theorists have not hesitated to suggest that all these 10^{500} types of universe must actually exist, constituting an immense multiversial 'landscape'. If that were the case, it might not perhaps be altogether surprising if one of them was our anthropically fruitful world. Yet the unrestrained speculation of such ontological prodigality seems wholly contrary to the scientific spirit. A much more economic metascientific option would be to see the world as a divine creation.

One further comment can be made before quitting this topic. It is somewhat ironic to note that if imposing conditions of mathematical consistency on relativistic quantum theory had turned out to lead to a unique theory without arbitrary parameters, the fact that its character, demanded by such abstract requirements, had led inexorably to an anthropically fruitful universe would surely have been the most astonishing coincidence of all.

Our attention now turns to the actual kind of developments that have taken place in the course of this universe's fruitful history, which over 13.7 billion years have turned what initially was an almost-uniform expanding ball of energy into the present-day home of scientists and saints. Science's understanding of the processes involved is that they have been evolutionary in character. This is not only true for the development of terrestrial life, but also for the universe itself, as galaxies and stars formed following the big bang. The expanding ball of matter/energy that was the immediate aftermath of the big bang was not completely uniform, for it contained some small fluctuations of density. Where there is more matter, there is more gravitational attraction, and so these fluctuations began to evolve into a lumpy cosmic structure, through a kind of snow-balling effect. Eventually, over a billion years, the resulting condensation made the universe grainy with galaxies and stars, an essential development since it was only in the stars that the heavier elements necessary for life could be formed.

The essence of evolutionary process, whether cosmic or terrestrial, is an interplay between two contrasting tendencies that in a slogan way may be called 'chance and necessity'. Chance stands for the contingent particularity of what actually happens, for example the particular pattern of those aboriginal fluctuations of density. The range of possibility is so great that only a small fraction of the events that might have happened have in fact occurred, even in the course of 13.7 billion years. Necessity stands for the underlying regularities of the world, including their anthropic specificity. In the case of star and galaxy formation, necessity would be the attractive law of gravity. It is from the interaction of these two factors of chance and necessity that true novelty emerges. A world that was pure chance would be too haphazard for anything new to be able to persist in it. A world that was pure necessity would be too rigid for anything to be possible beyond endless rearrangements of already existing structures. It is only in a world 'at the edge of chaos', where order and disorder, chance and necessity, interlace, that true contingent fertility is possible and genuinely new entities can emerge. The process is well exemplified by the story of biological evolution. If there were no genetic mutations (sheer necessity), there would be no new species. If there were endless genetic mutations (sheer chance), there would be no stable species on which natural selection could act. In our kind of world, the actual rate of mutation is such as to permit the development of interestingly novel forms of life, sifted and preserved through natural selection.

It is clear that the role of chance is not to be equated with meaninglessness, in the manner that Jacques Monod asserted.[9] Rather the role of chance is simply that of the contingent exploration of inherent potentialities for fruitfulness. Chance is no more than the happenstance of actual cosmic history. Monod also failed to acknowledge the very specific character that given necessity has to take in an anthropic universe if this exploration is to result in the evolved complexity of carbon-based life. The insights of evolutionary thinking are not hostile to seeing the world as God's creation, but they certainly provide a context which significantly shapes the resulting tone of theological discourse. It becomes clear that the Creator has chosen to act through unfolding process rather than by episodic intervention. The role of contingency indicates that this process is open towards its future. To use a musical metaphor that has been a favourite with Arthur Peacocke, an extensive and helpful writer on these topics,[10] the history of creation is to be seen, not as the performance of a fixed score already written in eternity, but as an unfolding improvisation in which creatures and their Creator both participate. We have considered earlier a kenotic understanding of creation in which God is seen to give the gift of due independence to creatures to be themselves and to 'make themselves' (as Charles Kingsley said in responding positively to Charles Darwin's evolutionary account of the development of life). That requires a world open in its character in a way that permits such creaturely exploration and improvisation. While the exact details of what has emerged in the course of cosmic history was not fixed from the start, nevertheless the presence of the deep potentiality built into the given fabric of created nature, of the kind that anthropic fine-tuning implies, indicates the universe to be a world of purposed fertility. Five-fingered homo sapiens was not decreed from the beginning, but it seems no accident that some form of self-conscious, God-conscious life has evolved. These insights encourage complementing the timeless concept of creatio ex nihilo with a temporal concept of unfolding creatio continua. The latter can be seen as characterised by the sequential emergence of new possibilities not previously realised, as when life emerged from inanimate matter, consciousness from life, and hominid self-consciousness from animal consciousness.[11] These novel developments need not be attributed to discontinous divine intervention, but rather they may be understood as new modes of manifestation of the inherent fruitfulness with which the Creator has endowed creation. The discussion of the spontaneous generation of holistic properties in complex systems, given in the preceding chapter, offers the prospect of a way to relate the insights of science to a theology of emergence in a mutually consonant manner.

A world of this evolving kind is a great good, reflecting the loving character of its Creator, displayed in the gift of a due degree of independence granted to creatures to be themselves and to make themselves. Many will see it as a greater good than a ready-made world would have been. Yet its fruitfulness has a necessary cost, a shadow side that cannot be avoided. Chance's shuffling explorations of potentiality will not only lead to fruitfulness, but they must also inevitably include ragged edges and blind alleys. Genetic mutation has been the engine driving biological evolution. In germ cells, mutation can lead to new forms of life; in somatic cells, mutation can lead to malignancy. The agonising fact of cancer is not gratuitous, something that a Creator who was a bit more competent, or a bit less callous, could easily have avoided. It is the necessary cost of a world in which creatures make themselves. An evolutionary creation has to be a world of transience, in which the death of one generation is the requisite for the new life of the next.

In this way, the context of science provides theology with some help in tackling its most profound and difficult perplexity: the problem of theodicy's struggle to understand the presence of disease and disaster in a world claimed to be the creation of a loving and powerful God. As science understands more and more about the processes of the world, it becomes clear that they are intricate and interlocking. What happens in nature cannot arbitrarily be torn apart and decomposed into parts that are good and parts that are bad, so that a benevolent Creator could readily have retained the good and eliminated the bad. It is all a package deal – think about the ambiguity of genetic mutation. Many other examples could be given. The existence of tectonic plates leads to earthquakes when they slip, but the gaps between the plates also allow mineral resources to well up from within the Earth, affording a necessary replenishment of its surface fertility. While this insight of the necessary integrity of natural process does not remove all perplexity – or anguish or anger – from our thinking about physical evil and suffering, it at least provides some degree of assistance that theology can draw upon from the context of science as it seeks to speak about the universe as God's creation.

The classic problem of theodicy was stated by Epicurus when he said that it seems that 'God either wishes to take away evils and is unable; or He is able and is unwilling'. The context of science encourages us to resolve this apparent clash between concepts of divine goodness and divine power by qualifying what is meant by God's being 'almighty'. It does not mean that God can do absolutely anything, but rather that God can do anything that is in accordance with the divine nature. God is not externally constrained, but God is internally constrained by the character of deity itself – the rational

God cannot decree that $2 + 2 = 5$. The God whose nature is love cannot be the Cosmic Tyrant whose creation is no more than a divine puppet theatre, its creatures inexorably responding to the pull of every string. Creatures must be allowed to be themselves and to make themselves. The well-known 'free-will defence' asserts, as a response to the existence of moral evil, that a world with creatures able to make moral choices, whether for good or ill, is a better world than would be one populated by perfectly programmed automata. In response to the existence of the physical evils of disease and disaster, one may make a corresponding 'free-process defence', claiming that a world whose evolving nature is granted its own integrity – a gift resulting in both great fruitfulness and an unavoidable cost of suffering and malformation – is a better world than one in which a capricious magic is continually at work to avoid unpleasant effects.[12] Only in a world sufficiently consistent in its character for deeds to have foreseeable consequences, could moral choice and responsibility be exercised. The two 'defences' are intimately related to each other. I suspect that only a universe to whose physical fabric the free-process defence applied could give rise to beings to whom the free-will defence applies.

Providence

In the eighteenth century, it seemed to many as if Newtonian science had produced the picture of a world of mere mechanism. Julien Offray de La Mettrie even went so far as to write a book entitled *Man the Machine*. If there were to be a God for such a world, that deity could be no more than a deistic Spectator, who had decreed the laws of nature and then simply stepped aside to observe the inevitable unfolding of their consequences.

We have seen already that twentieth-century science, with its discovery of the intrinsic unpredictabilities present in physical process, brought about the demise of a merely mechanical picture of physical reality. It thus became possible to espouse a metaphysical interpretation of process that was capable of accommodating the operation of holistic causal principles of a pattern-forming kind, acting in addition to those exchanges of energy between constituents which till then had made up science's sole account. I have argued in the last chapter that an understanding of nature thus became available that was consonant with our experience of the exercise of human agency.

One could take science seriously without being driven to Mettrie's absurdity of human automata.

Moreover, it was also possible, using the idea of some form of genuine top-down causality, to find a hint of how it might be that divine providence could also be understood to be at work in history, shaping its unfolding development through the input of some generalised form of information into the open grain of nature. One could recognise this idea as being one that was broadly consonant with the theological concept of God's Spirit, actively but hiddenly at work within creation's history. It is important to recognise that what was proposed was not arbitrary supernatural intervention from outside of nature, of an episodic or even magical character, but continuous divine interaction within the created openness of the natural world. To take an expression from a related topic in theology, gracious providence was to be conceived as completing nature, not displacing it.

In seeking to explore these possibilities, different people focused initially on different loci of intrinsic unpredictability, some looking to quantum indeterminacy and others to chaotic uncertainty.[13] None of these attempted models should be taken with undue detailed seriousness. They are what a physicist would call 'thought experiments', attempts to explore and try out ideas in a simplified way, rather than purporting to be complete solutions to the problem of divine action. Questions of agency are too complex and profound to be answered adequately by simple suppositions, such as the notion that God and/or human beings act simply through the direct exploitation of quantum uncertainty or the direct manipulation of non-linear chaotic systems. Agency must surely involve much more subtle and interlocking processes than this, acting at a variety of levels and of a greater complexity than such localised accounts could possibly describe. Yet the thought experiments were worthwhile. We have recognised earlier that the idea of top-down causality, though intuitively appealing because of our actual experience of agency, is not unproblematic scientifically. Its plausibility demands some form of causal analysis, however tentative, to indicate that there is genuine room for its operation. If causality were saturated by bottom-up effects alone (as in Kauffman's computer model), there would be no scope for genuine top-down effectiveness. Interpreting intrinsic unpredictabilities as signs of ontological openness to the operation of other causal principles affords just such necessary room for manoeuvre. So an important point was being made by this exploratory work. We have already noted also that science's account of the causal structure of the world is not only potentially open to a future that it cannot predict, but it is also patchy in its character. Different domains of the physical world, such as the microscopic regime of quantum theory and the macroscopic regime of classical physics, relate to each other in ways that currently are not fully understood.[14] For example, we have seen that quantum physics and chaotic physics do not fit compatibly together, since the former has an intrinsic scale set by Planck's constant (which gives a meaning to 'small' or 'large'), while the fractal nature of chaos means that it is scale-free (it looks the same at whatever size it is sampled). Claims to establish the complete causal closure of the physical world of the kind that a reductive physicalism makes, simply cannot be sustained. While we are not in a position to identify uniquely and exhaustively the causal joints by which agency might be exercised, taking the context of science seriously does not demand that we deny the possibility of such agency, either human or divine.

Many theologians rightly recognise that providential action is properly to be understood in terms of a continuing divine interaction with creation, rather than in the disruptive terms of episodic divine intervention. God who is the Ordainer of nature will surely work within the open grain of natural process, and not against that grain. To suppose the contrary would be to risk the theological absurdity of a contradiction between the God who wills the order of nature and the same God who acts in nature's history. At the very least, the discussion of divine action within the science and theology community can claim to have succeeded in removing that particular threat of theological incoherence. However, the context of science does suggest to theology some constraints that it should respect in its picture of the operation of divine providential action.

First, while there is certainly much widespread cloudy unpredictability in the world, there is also a good deal of clockwork predictability as well. Either through the mutual averaging out of quantum fluctuations among the constituents of large systems, or through the robustness possessed by many macroscopic systems, of a kind that makes them impervious to the effects of the infinitesimal environmental disturbances that might otherwise trigger chaotic behaviour, there are many examples of predictable behaviour to be found in nature. There are 'clocks' as well as 'clouds'. Science could not have developed if there had not been large regimes of reliable predictability open to investigation. These regularities have frequently been interpreted theologically as signs of the Creator's faithfulness, for example in the reliable succession of the seasons. There is no reason to expect them to be set aside. Consequently there are some outcomes which it does not make sense to pray for. Origen recognised this in the third century when he said that one should not pray for the cool of spring in the heat of summer, tempting though it must have been to do so in his native Alexandria. God's special providence cannot be expected to be exercised just to relieve the sweaty discomfort of the believer. The question of whether nevertheless there might be highly non-trivial circumstances in which the Ordainer of nature might fittingly act in unprecedented, and so naturally inexplicable, ways is the question of miracle, to which we shall return in the next chapter. A key question will be how one may understand the miraculous in a way that clearly shows it to be divine action that is meaningful and not capricious.

Second, if providence normally acts within the cloudy unpredictabilities of the world, then its presence will not be unambiguously demonstrable, even if it may be discernible by the eye of faith. The process of the world cannot be dissected and itemised, allocating this event to nature, that event to human agency, and a third event to divine providence. The character of what happens is too intricately entangled and veiled from detailed view for this to be possible. A watcher on the edges of the Reed Sea can observe the appearance of a band of fleeing slaves, hotly pursued by soldiers. He can see a wind start up, temporarily driving back the waters and allowing the fugitives to cross the marsh. He can note that the wind then drops and the waters return, engulfing the pursuers. That spectator cannot be obliged to interpret this as more than an amazingly fortunate coincidence. But one of the fleeing Israelites cannot be forbidden to see the event as part of God's great act of deliverance from slavery in Egypt. The context of science is too limited in its explanatory scope to be able to afford a means to adjudicate such claims for theological significance.

Finally, one should note that classical theology would repudiate the whole tenor of this discussion. Its account of divine action invokes the concept of a primary causality, ineffably at work in and under the network of secondary causalities exercised by creatures. God is never to be thought of as acting as a cause among causes, in the manner of the discussion given above. In reply, one could suggest that the kenosis involved in creation has included just such a divine condescension to be present to creation in this mode, a kind of cosmic counterpart of the local and historically specific kenotic condescension of the Word made flesh in the incarnation.

Relationality

The context of physical science in the nineteenth century was largely atomistic. Great progress had been made in understanding chemical reactions by thinking in terms of molecules made out of the atoms of the elements of the periodic table. Kinetic theory had achieved great success in explaining heat and other bulk properties in terms of molecular motion. All this had served to strengthen the Newtonian picture of physical process expressed in terms of the interactions of discrete constituents, moving in the container of absolute space and in the course of the unfolding of absolute time. In the second half of the century, Maxwell's theory of the electromagnetic field had employed the different concept of an entity extended in space, but even here fields had local properties, since there was no instantaneous correlation of changes in the field taking place at different points. Things could change 'here' without inducing immediate consequences elsewhere. The general picture remained that of a natural world that could be considered bit by separate bit. By the beginning of the twenty-first century, however, this understanding had been modified very substantially.

Albert Einstein's successive great discoveries of special and general relativity showed that space, time, and matter are intimately related in a single package deal. Matter curves the geometry of space-time and that curvature, in turn, deflects the paths of matter. Quantum theory has demonstrated the presence of a deep-seated relationality present in the subatomic world (the so-called 'EPR effect'). Once two quantum entities have interacted, they become so mutually entangled that effectively they constitute a single system, however far apart they may separate spatially.[15] Acting on one 'here' has an instantaneous effect on the other, even if it is very distant – 'beyond the moon' as we conventionally say. Einstein thought that this effect was too 'spooky' to be true, but clever experiments have shown that non-locality ('togetherness-in-separation') is indeed a property of nature.[16] Elementary particles such as electrons are not totally separate from each other, for they are excitations in a single electron field and they exert a mutual influence through what the physicists call 'statistics', so that, for example, there is an exclusion principle requiring that no two electrons can be in exactly the same state of motion.

On a macroscopic scale, we have seen that dissipative systems that are held far from thermal equilibrium by the exchange of energy and entropy with their environment, display astonishing and wholly unexpected powers of self-organisation, spontaneously generating remarkable holistic patterns of long-range dynamical behaviour. Chaos theory exhibits the widespread existence of systems of such exquisite sensitivity to the minutest detail of their circumstances that they cannot effectively be isolated from the influences of their environment. Thus it has turned out that even the ordinary physics of the everyday world is more subtle and inter-relational than generations of Newtonian thinkers had been able to discern.

The scientific and metascientific consequences of these manifold discoveries of relationality are still being worked out, but it is clear that our commonsense experience of the apparent separability of objects is more problematic than one would previously have thought. Science's methodological strategy of reductionism – 'Divide and Rule' – is only partially successful. Complex entities possess holistic properties that are unforeseeable and inexplicable in terms of a purely constituent analysis.[17] As the saying goes, 'More is different', the whole exceeds the sum of its parts.

This scientific discovery that 'Reality is relational' will come as no surprise in the context of Christian theology, whose trinitarian thinking has long known the truth of 'Being as Communion'.[18] In the unity of the Godhead there is the eternal exchange of love between the three divine Persons, the mutual relationality of the interpenetration of love that the theologians call perichoresis. The relational context of science does not of itself shed new light on this theological mystery, and even less does it demonstrate its necessary truth, but science's picture of the physical world is strikingly consonant with a belief that that world is the creation of the triune God.[19] It is also consonant with Christian belief in the interconnection of the faithful as they are united as members of the body of Christ.

There is a further point of meeting between science and religion, when both seek to speak about the future history of the universe. Science predicts that after very many billions of years, all will end in futility, most probably through the long drawn out decay of a world becoming steadily colder and more dilute. Certainly, carbon-based life cannot be expected to be more than a transient episode in cosmic history. Theology asserts that the end of history will lie in the coming of the Kingdom of God. There is no immediate and simple consonance between these two prognoses. The problem that this poses is sufficiently important to demand later treatment of its own in chapter 7.

6

Motivated belief

As we noted earlier, scientists are not inclined to subscribe to an a priori concept of what is reasonable. They have found the physical world to be too surprising, too resistant to prior expectation, for a simple trust in human powers of rational prevision to be at all persuasive. Instead, the actual character of our encounter with reality has to be allowed to shape our knowledge and thought about the object of our enquiry. Different levels of reality may be expected to have their idiosyncratic characters, and there will not be a single epistemic rule for all. A physicist, aware of the counterintuitive natures of the quantum world and of cosmic curved space-time, is not tempted to make commonsense the sole measure of rational expectation. Because of this, we have seen that the instinctive question for the scientist to ask is not 'Is it reasonable?', as if one knew beforehand the shape that rationality had to take, but 'What makes you think that might be the case?' Radical revision of expectation cannot be ruled out, but it will only be accepted if evidence is presented in support of the new point of view that is being proposed. Science trades in motivated belief.

One of the difficulties that face a scientist wanting to speak to his colleagues about the Christian faith is to get across the fact that theology also trades in motivated belief. Many scientists are both wistful and wary in their attitude towards religion. They can see that science's story is not sufficient by itself to give a satisfying account of the many-layered reality of the world. Those who acknowledge this are open to a search for wider and deeper understanding. Hence the wistful desire for something beyond science. Religion offers such a prospect, but many scientists fear that it does so on unacceptable terms. Their wariness arises from the mistaken idea that religious faith demands that those who embrace it should be willing to believe simply on the basis of submission to some unquestionable authority – the claimed utterances of a divine being, the unchallengeable assertions of a sacred book, the authoritative decrees of a controlling community, whatever it may be – simply declared to be unproblematic deliverances of infallible truth. The picture that many scientists have of religious revelation is that it is a collection of non-negotiable propositions, presented to be accepted without further argument or attempt at justification. According to this view, faith is simply a matter of signing on the dotted line without taking too much care about the small print. These scientists fear that religious belief would demand of them an act of intellectual suicide. I believe this to be a quite disastrous misconception. If an uncritical fideism is what religious belief requires, then I would have the greatest difficulty in being a religious person. What I am always trying to do in conversation with my not-yet-believing friends is to show them that I have motivations for my religious beliefs, just as I have motivations for my scientific beliefs. They may not share my view of the adequacy of these motivations, but at least they should recognise that they are there on offer as matters for rational consideration and assessment. Theology conducted in the context of science must be prepared to be candid about the evidence for its beliefs. This task is one of great importance, since the difficulty of getting a hearing for Christian faith in contemporary society often seems to stem from the fact that many people have never given adequate adult consideration to the possibility of its being true, thinking that they 'know' already that there can be no truth in claims so apparently at odds with notions of everyday secular expectation.

While science and religion share a common concern for motivated belief, the character of the motivating evidence is, of course, different in the two cases. We have already explored some of these differences in chapter 2. Theology lacks recourse to repeatable experimental confirmation ('Do not put the Lord your God to the test', Deuteronomy 6:16), as in fact do most other non-scientific explorations of reality. Judgements such as that of the quality of a painting, or the beauty of a piece of music, or the character of a friend, depend upon powers of sympathetic discernment, rather than being open to empirical demonstration. Moreover, I have already said that I believe that no form of human truth-seeking enquiry can attain absolute certainty about its conclusions. The realistic aspiration is that of attaining the best explanation of complex phenomena, a goal to be achieved by searching for an understanding sufficiently comprehensive and well-motivated as to afford the basis for rational commitment. Neither science nor religion can entertain the hope of establishing logically coercive proof of the kind that only a fool could deny. No one can avoid some degree of intellectual precariousness, and there is a consequent need for a degree of cautious daring in the quest for truth. Experience and interpretation intertwine in an inescapable circularity. Even science cannot wholly escape this dilemma (theory interprets experiments; experiments confirm or disconfirm theories). We have seen how considerations of this kind led Michael Polanyi to acknowledge the presence of a tacit dimension in scientific practice, depending on the exercise of skills of judgement, and to speak of science as necessarily being personal knowledge, not absolutely certain but still capable of eliciting justified belief. Recall that he said that he wrote *Personal Knowledge* to explain how he might commit himself to what he believed (scientifically) to be true, while knowing that it might be false. This stance recognises what I believe to be the unavoidable epistemic condition of humanity.

When we turn to religious belief, it too cannot lay claim to certainty beyond a peradventure – for believers live by faith and not by sight. Yet faith is by no means the irrational acceptance of unquestionable propositions. I believe my religious faith to be well-motivated and that is why, for me, Christianity is worthy of acceptance and commitment. Religious people are content to bet their lives that this is so. If theology is to prove persuasive to enquirers in the context of science, it will have to set out the motivations for the assertions that it makes, expressed in as honest and careful a fashion as possible. I believe that the argument will need to have the character of bottom-up thinking, making appeal to specific forms of evidence.

There are two broad kinds of motivation for religious belief. One looks to certain general aspects of the human encounter with reality, while the other approach focuses on particularities of personal experience, including what are understood to have been specific acts of divine disclosure expressed through uniquely significant events and persons. The first kind of motivation includes the concerns of natural theology, presented as a ground for general theistic belief. We have already given some attention to this topic. By itself, natural theology can lead only to a rather abstract concept of deity, as consistent with the spectatorial god of deism as it is with the active God of theism. The considerations presented in the last chapter went beyond this aspect in order to seek enriched theological insight, of a kind capable of including the concepts of unfolding continuous creation and divine providential interaction with history. However, only obliquely, through the recognition of relationality, did the argument of that chapter make contact with the defining specificities of Christian faith. For that purpose one has to have recourse to the second kind of motivation for religious beliefs.

This latter approach is the concern of revealed theology, presented as the ground for the beliefs of a particular faith tradition. In this chapter I want to give concise consideration to how one might formulate such an approach to Christian belief. An adequate treatment would require extensive discussion and, in a modest way, that is a task that I have attempted elsewhere.[1] Here my purpose is simply to sketch enough of the argument to illustrate and support the claim that theology does indeed trade in motivated belief and that it can present its insights in a manner fitting for consideration in the context of science. Addressing this task will serve to indicate how Christian believers may best commend their faith in an intellectual setting in which thinking is much influenced by the successes of science. Recent high-profile attacks on religious belief by some scientists have made much play of depicting believers as if they were simple-minded fideists of an anti-intellectual mindset.[2] The demolition of such strawmen is an unworthy polemical strategy. Christian theology's pursuit of motivated belief demonstrates the misleading character of this kind of antireligious argument.

In earlier chapters we looked in some detail at the arguments that natural theology can deploy. The deep and wonderful order of the world was pointed to as being suggestive of a divine Mind expressed in creation. The anthropic fine-tuning that enabled an initial ball of energy to develop into the home of saints and scientists was interpreted as being suggestive of a divine Purpose at work in cosmic history. Other arguments of natural theology suggested that the existence of value, both moral and aesthetic, is best explained in terms of human intuitions of God's good and perfect will and of human participation in the Creator's joy in creation.[3] These are not knock-down arguments – there are no such arguments, either for theism or for atheism – but they do offer insightful and satisfying ways to gain an enhanced understanding of the richness of human experience. However, even if they are granted maximal persuasiveness, these general kinds of consideration can only lead to a generic concept of God, conceived in such terms as deity thought of as Cosmic Mind or the Ground of Value. They can serve to put the question of the existence of God onto the agenda of enquiry, but they necessarily leave unanswered many questions concerning what the nature of that God might actually be. For example, does God really care for individual human beings? Any attempt to answer that question has to look to something more specific than general experience. My own religious belief is in the God and Father of our Lord Jesus Christ. I want to outline the motivations that I believe support my Christian faith, living and thinking as I do in the context of modern science, so different in many ways to the context in which Christianity began two millennia ago. It would not be enough for me to rest content with the God of natural theology, who is too distant a kind of deity, corresponding in nature to the rather abstract arguments concerning order and value invoked in support of this kind of belief. Einstein possessed a kind of cosmic religiosity, inspired by the wonderful order of the universe, but he was emphatic that he did not believe in a personal God.[4]

To find such a God he would have had to be willing to look elsewhere, beyond the austere insights of fundamental physics. Belief in a deity who is properly to be spoken of in personal terms, however stretched the meaning of those terms must necessarily be, has to be motivated differently, by reference to particular events and persons, understood as affording revelatory disclosures of unique and unrepeatable significance. It is precisely this specificity of divine action and communication that makes the personal language of Father appropriate in Christian discourse, rather than the impersonal language of Force, which would carry the implication of an unchanging mode of divine expression, unrelated to any particularities of person or situation, just like the unyielding law of gravity. We shall return to this matter when discussing the issue of miracle.

These considerations underline how essential it is to have a right understanding of the nature of revelation. What is involved is not the mysterious deposit of infallible information, conveyed in an incomprehensible and unchallengeable fashion, but rather it is the record of those particularly transparent occasions that have been open to an exceptional degree to the discernment of the divine will and presence. Christian theology accords a normative status to the Bible precisely because it contains an irreplaceable account of God's dealing with God's chosen people, the Israelites, and the uniquely significant history of the life, death, and resurrection of Jesus of Nazareth. One might say that scripture functions as the 'laboratory notebook' containing the record of these 'critical observations' of divine self-disclosure. Its role is not that of the authoritative text-book in which one can conveniently look up all the ready-made answers. Scripture is something more subtle and more powerful than that.[5] There are many different modes in which the Bible can be read, and one of the most important of these is simply as providing moti-vating evidence for Christian belief. This is a theme on which I have written a number of times, most extensively in my Gifford Lectures.[6] In this chapter I want to sketch an outline of how the careful and scrupulous study of the New Testament can provide the reasons why I believe that Christian belief does indeed correspond to what is the case. I shall seek to offer the argument in the evidence-based manner that seems consistent with taking seriously the context of sci-ence within which Christian belief has to be expressed and defended today.

The writings of the New Testament originated in a particular part of the ancient world and they were written over a specific period of some forty years or so. They are very diverse in their character. Three of the major authors involved, Paul, John and the unknown Writer of the Epistle to the Hebrews, display a depth of theological origin-ality and understanding that secures for them a permanent place of creative influence in the history of Christian thought. Much of the writing in the New Testament has the occasional character associated with letters, but other parts are more systematic in construction, including four examples of what was then a novel kind of literature, gospels, whose accounts of Jesus of Nazareth are shaped by the authors' desire to proclaim the good news of God's salvific purposes, which they believe have been made known and accomplished in him. It is important to recognise that the gospels are not modern biographies written in the detached manner of scientific historiog-raphy. They are interpreted accounts of a remarkable man, and they are intent on making clear the meaning of what the authors believe was happening in what had been going on in his life, death, and its aftermath. No scientist could deny the importance of proper interpretation if true significance is to be discerned. Raw data (readings in counters, marks on photographic plates) are insufficient by themselves to tell a story of evident interest.

Jesus had a comparatively short public ministry, but it had enormous local impact, drawing crowds who were anxious to hear his words and who often sought the healing ministry that he exercised. Then, on a last visit to Jerusalem, it all seemed to fall apart. The authorities, civil (Roman) and religious (Jewish) acting together, moved in to avoid trouble. Jesus was arrested and hastily executed, suffering the painful and shameful fate of crucifixion, the kind of death reserved for slaves and rebels and seen by pious Jews as being a sign of God's rejection ('any one hung on a tree is under God's curse', Deuteronomy 21:23). Except for a few staunch women, his followers ran away, overcome by despair and disappointment. From the place of execution there came the cry 'My God, my God, why have you forsaken me?' (Matthew 27:46; Mark 15:34). On the face of it, Jesus' death seems a moment of pathetic failure, the final disillusionment of the followers of a rejected man whose grand pretensions had suddenly and definitively been found wanting. If that really was the end of the story of Jesus, I believe that most of us would never have heard of him. At best he would have seemed to be no better than other first-century messianic pretenders whose causes also finally failed. So the first remarkable thing about Jesus is that he is known to all of us. We need to look closer into the New Testament to find out why, against all reasonable expectation, his story continued beyond his death.

Amid the variety of its component writings, there are certain common themes that recur in the New Testament. Three of the most important themes are:

1 All the writers believe that the story of Jesus continued because God raised him from the dead on the third day after his crucifixion. We shall have to pay further attention to this extraordinary claim, but the existence of the New Testament, and the character of its contents, are unintelligible without the recognition that this is what its writers are affirming.

2 In wrestling with what they believe to be their experience of the risen Christ, the writers are driven, in their different ways, to speak of Jesus in a quite extraordinary manner. They know that

he was a man living in Palestine in their own times, yet in the accounts they give they often seem driven to employ not only obvious human categories, but also to use language that is only appropriate to deity. The Pauline epistles are probably of the earliest Christian writings known to us, certainly antedating the gospels. Already Jesus of Nazareth is being referred to in remarkable terms. Paul begins almost all his letters with some such phrase as 'Grace to you and peace from God our Father and the Lord Jesus Christ' (Romans 1:7; 1 Corinthians 1:3; and so on). Not only is Jesus being bracketed with God in a manner that would, for example, have been inappropriate for a pious Jew to use in relation to Moses, the servant of God, but he is also accorded the title 'Lord'. While this word, *kyrios*, had a widespread secular usage amounting to no more than politeness of address, its Hebrew counterpart, *adonai*, also had a special Jewish religious usage as an acceptable circumlocution in place of the unutterable divine name, YHWH, a particular significance which the religious context of Paul's greeting could scarcely fail to invoke. The gospel of John portrays Jesus as claiming unity with God (John 10:30, words uttered in a situation where the hostile crowd are shown as having no difficulty in detecting what they see as the blasphemous implication), and it assigns to Jesus the use of images (the bread of life, the true vine, and so on) which carry implications of more than human status. The Writer to the Hebrews proclaims that 'in these last days [God] has spoken to us by a Son, whom he appointed the heir of all things and through whom he also created the worlds' (Hebrews 1:2). Examples could easily be multiplied. It is clear that when it comes to Jesus, the New Testament writers cannot rest content with the standard Jewish repertoire for speaking of people with special gifts from God – the categories of prophet, teacher, healer – but, against all their instincts as monotheistic Jews, they are driven to use divine-sounding language about him. Remember that they are referring to a near contemporary, and not to some shadowy figure of a legendary past. The New Testament very seldom out and out calls Jesus God (the confession of Thomas in John 20:28 is perhaps the clearest example), but its pages manifest a continual tension between the use of human and divine manners of speaking about him. The problem thus posed is unresolved in the New Testament itself, but succeeding

Christian generations had to address it and eventually the Church was led to the distinctive and extraordinary doctrinal concept of the incarnation, the affirmation of the presence of deity in the life of this first-century Jew, who truly was the Son of God.

3 Coupled with this recourse to divine language, and fuelling its fire, was a firm conviction among those first-generation Christians that the risen Christ had brought into their lives a new and transforming experience of saving power. Paul wrote to the Corinthinians, 'if anyone is in Christ, there is a new creation: everything old has passed away; see everything has become new!' (2 Corinthians 5:17). I believe that an adequate Christology (a true understanding of the nature of Jesus) must satisfy the criterion of affording an adequate soteriology (a true understanding of the power of Christ in human lives, to which the Church has continued to give its testimony down through the centuries). The doctrine of the incarnation implies that in the Word made flesh a unique bridge was established between the created life of humanity and the uncreated life of God, and in this meeting of divine power and human nature there lies a way of understanding the fulfilment of the soteriological criterion.

These three lines of testimony need to be presented for consideration by anyone seeking to understand the significance that Jesus of Nazareth holds for Christian belief. In the context of science the discussion of the persuasiveness of that belief cannot be conducted satisfactorily without a detailed engagement with these claims. The task is indispensable to honest enquiry and it is made all the more important today by the fact that many people seem to have so little knowledge of what the New Testament actually says. The pivot on which the claim of a unique and transcendent significance for Jesus must turn is clearly the resurrection. If in fact he was raised from the dead to a new and unending life of glory, then it is indeed credible that he has an altogether unique status and role in salvation history. If, sadly, his life ended in failure and his body was left to moulder in the grave, then he seems at best little different from many other prophetic figures who have suffered martyrdom for holding fast to the integrity of their beliefs. The quest for motivated Christian faith has to begin by focusing on the question of the resurrection. I believe that it would be a serious apologetic mistake if Christian theology thought that operating in the context of science should somehow discourage it from laying proper emphasis on the essential centrality of Christ's resurrection, however counterintuitive that belief may seem in the light of mundane expectation.

As a preliminary, one must first face the general issue of miracle. It was as clear in the first century as it is today, that it is wholly contrary to any reasonable natural expectation that a man should be resurrected within history. While there were parties in first-century Judaism which expected a general resurrection at the end of history, none expected the resurrection of a specific person to take place within history, even if there was some hope that a prophetic figure, such as Elijah, might have been stored up in heaven in order to be returned for a further spell of earthly life at some critical juncture in Jewish history. It is important here to recognise the distinction between resuscitation and resurrection. The former applies to someone like Lazarus, who is portrayed in John's gospel as being called out of the tomb after an apparent death (John 11), but who was undoubtedly expected by all to die again in due course. Resuscitation is only a temporary reprieve from mortality. Resurrection, on the other hand, implies a transition from this mortal life to a new form of glorified life, lived without end in the presence of God. Resurrection is a permanent victory over mortality. The possibility of resurrection lies wholly outside the context of scientific explanation. If the resurrection of Jesus happened, it could only have been through a special exercise of divine power. In short, resurrection is, in the strict sense of the word, a miracle.

The real problem of belief in miracle is properly a theological issue, not a scientific one, since claims of unique historical occurrences lie outside science's competence to adjudicate. All it can do is reinforce the commonsense recognition that something like a resurrection does not usually happen. The real challenge to belief in miracle lies elsewhere. It is theologically inconceivable that God should act capriciously as a kind of celestial conjurer, doing a turn today that God did not think of doing yesterday and won't be bothered to do tomorrow. The theological problem of miracle is that of discerning divine consistency in the face of a claim of radically novel action. How that consistency is understood depends upon a proper understanding of what is involved in speaking of God in personal terms. I have already said that divine action is not to be assimilated to a kind of impersonal and unchanging process, similar to that which characterises the law of gravity. If personal language is to mean anything when used about God, it must imply a divine freedom to respond in particular and different ways to particular and different situations, including even the rational possibility of unprecedented action in unprecedented circumstances. Once again we encounter the unavoidable necessity of hermeneutic circularity. Of course, persons are not normally resurrected in history, but if there is something truly unique about Jesus (the Son of God), then his story could conceivably have included unique events. Equally, if he was resurrected, this was surely a sign that he indeed did have an altogether unique status. However, if he was just another prophet, then the story of his resurrection is likely to be no more than a touching legend. Both possibilities have to be considered. To believe in the resurrection rightly requires significant motivating evidence, a question to which we shall turn shortly, but its possibility should not be ruled out absolutely from the beginning, before even considering what evidence there might be for this counterintuitive belief. Moreover, it is important to note that the Christian understanding of Christ's resurrection is that it occurred within history as the unique seed event from which a resurrected destiny for all people will come about beyond history ('for as all die in Adam, so all will be made alive in Christ'; 1 Corinthians 15:22). In this sense, what Christian theology sees as unique about the resurrection is its timing, rather than its occurrence. Further consideration will be given to this point in the succeeding chapter.

So what evidence could there be? I have already argued that something must have happened to continue the story of Jesus, and it seems to me that after that devastating arrest and execution, it must have been something much more than simply a return of nerve on the part of the disciples, coupled with a resolve to try to continue to recall the life and words of their Master. The New Testament sets out two lines of evidence in support of its much stronger claim. One of these is the sequence of stories relating to encounters with the risen Christ taking place after his death. The earliest such account available to us is the list of witnesses, most of them then still living, given by Paul in 1 Corinthians 15:3–11. The letter itself was probably written some twenty to twenty-five years after the crucifixion, but its reference to what Paul himself 'had received' (v. 3) seems naturally to imply that he is repeating what he had been taught following his dramatic conversion on the road to Damascus, which would take the quoted testimony back to within two or three years of the events themselves.

To get some feel of what these encounters with the risen Christ might have been like, one has to turn to the gospels. The appearance stories there related vary in their detail and location, but there is a common theme, differently expressed in the different stories but persistently present, namely that initially it was difficult to recognise who it was who had been encountered. Mary Magdalene at first supposes the risen Jesus to be the gardener (John 20:15); the couple on the road to Emmaus are unaware who their companion is until the final moment of parting (Luke 24:16); Matthew (28:17) even frankly admits that on a Galilean hillside some of the crowd doubted it was him; and so on. Most of the stories focus on a disclosure moment when it suddenly becomes apparent, against all expectation, that it is Jesus who is there. This seems a most unlikely feature to recur if the stories were just a bunch of tales, variously made up by various people in various places and for various purposes. I believe that this difficulty of recognition is a genuine historical reminiscence of what those encounters were actually like, and I take their evidence correspondingly seriously. Because the context of science lays emphasis on human embodiment, I believe that the true humanity of the risen Christ implies that these appearances would not have been some form of shared visionary experience, but they involved a corporeal presence, though necessarily of a transformed kind, as Christ's power of sudden appearance and disappearance makes clear.[7]

The second line of evidence presented relates to the discovery of the empty tomb. Here there is a good deal of similarity between the accounts in all the four gospels, even if there are minor discrepancies about such details as the exact time of early morning when the discovery was made and what were the exact names of the women involved. Such variations are not surprising in an account which had an oral history before attaining its various written forms. It is striking that the first reaction reported of the women is fear. The empty tomb is not treated as being self-explanatory, an instant knock-down proof of resurrection. It needs interpretation. Here, as in the appearance stories, there is a notable absence of any facile triumphalism. Rather, there is a sense of awe and mystery at an unanticipated great act of God.

But was there actually a tomb? We know that the bodies of exe-cuted felons were frequently cast by the Romans into a common and anonymous grave, or even left to be eaten by wild animals. Yet it is also known from archaeological evidence that this was not an in-variable practice, and the first-century Jewish historian Josephus tells us that his religion's burial customs required proper interment on the day of death even for executed malefactors. The association of Jesus' burial with the action of the otherwise unknown Joseph of Arimathea strengthens the case for belief in an identifiable tomb, since there seems to be no obvious reason to assign Joseph this hon-ourable role unless he actually performed it. In subsequent contro-versies between Jews and Christians, which can be traced back into the first century, there is a common acceptance that there was a tomb, with the disagreement being whether it was empty because Jesus had risen or because the disciples had stolen the body in an act of deceit. Even more strongly one can say that there would have seemed to be no reason at all to associate the story of this astonishing dis-covery with women, considered unreliable witnesses in the ancient world, unless in fact they were the ones who were actually involved in making it.

These matters demand much more detailed discussion than it has been appropriate to lay out here. The New Testament testimony is certainly complex in its character. As is often the case with import-ant historical issues, the available evidence is not such as must inevitably lead to a single conclusion with which all can be expected to concur without any question of dissent. In the particular case of the resurrection, all I have tried to do is briefly to indicate that there is important evidence to which the Christian believer can point in giving a positive answer to the question 'What makes you think that the resurrection of Jesus is, in fact, the case?' I believe that all truth-seeking people should be willing to consider this evidence seriously. I do not pretend that in the end all will turn out to weigh that evi-dence in the same way that I do. There are many less focused con-siderations that will influence judgement about so significant and counterintuitive a matter. Those with an unrevisable commitment to the sufficiency of a reductionist naturalism will follow David Hume and simply refuse to countenance the possibility of the miraculous, whatever the alleged evidence. Those of us who are Christians will be influenced in our conclusions by what we affirm to be our contemporary experience of the hidden but real presence of the risen Christ, encountered in sacramental worship. What I do claim is that Christian theology can be open and willing to accept the challenge to offer motivations for its beliefs, in the spirit that is so natural when that theology is being done in the context of science. In that context, detailed historical analysis of the kind that N. T. Wright gives in *The Resurrection of the Son of God*[8] is much to be welcomed. Some theologians seem more concerned with the conceptual motifs that they detect in the stories than with questions of historicity. In fact, both types of consideration are surely necessary. There has to be a metanarrative, a myth expressing theological significance, but if the doctrine of the incarnation truly fuses the power of a symbolic story with the power of an historically true story, then both these dimensions of significance have to be treated with integrity and respect. The Christian myth is claimed to be an enacted myth, and there is evidence to motivate that claim.

I believe that when the truth of Christianity is under consideration in the context of science, it is with these issues relating to the resurrection that the discussion needs to begin. Only when a case has been made for the belief that God was present in Jesus of Nazareth in a unique way, does it then become possible adequately to attempt to enquire into the significance of his crucifixion. The doctrine of the incarnation implies that in the spectacle of that deserted figure hanging on the cross, God is seen to be more than just a compassionate spectator of the travail of creation, looking down upon it in pity from the invulnerability of heaven. If the incarnation is true, then God in Christ has truly been a fellow-participant in the suffering of the world, knowing it from the inside. The Christian God is the crucified God.[9] In this profound insight, Christian faith meets the challenge of theodicy at the deep level that it demands.

A second Christian insight into the significance of Christ's crucifixion has focused the conviction that 'he died for our sins in accordance with the scriptures' (1 Corinthians 15:3). The reconciliation of estranged humanity to God across the bridge of the incarnation joining the created to the divine, which brought about that experience of new life to which the New Testament writers testify, was a costly transaction involving the death of the Son of God. This has been the Church's conviction from the earliest times, but no single and universally agreed upon theological theory, accounting for the full significance of what was going on in that great act of atonement, has come to be accepted in the Christian community. In a situation not without its parallels in science (for example in parts of nuclear physics and condensed matter physics), there have been many models of atonement (as various as the propitiation of an affronted God, a mythic victory over the Powers of darkness, and the exemplary force of sacrificial love, to mention only a few), but no comprehensive theory. Neither in science nor theology is failure to attain a fully articulated explanatory understanding a reason for denying the truth of the experience itself.

The approach that we have been following in seeking an evidence-motivated understanding of the significance of Jesus Christ is what the theologians call 'Christology from below'. Not only is it the natural route to follow in the context of science, but it is also one that can be seen a posteriori to be theologically appropriate in the light of the doctrine of the incarnation. If God indeed acted to make known the divine nature most clearly and accessibly through the human life of the incarnate Son of God, then the historical study of that life must be a matter of the greatest importance. Of course, there has been endless argument concerning how accessible the historical Jesus can actually be to modern study. Some think that the New Testament records are so shaped and influenced by the ideas and experiences of the earliest Christians that one can hardly penetrate beyond them to gain access to the one of whom they claim to speak. According to this view, it is only the 'Christ of faith', preached in the initial Christian communities, who can be known to us today. I resist so sharp a separation between the life of Jesus and the preached faith that life inspired. Of course there has been continual and developing reflection upon Jesus from the first generation of his followers until today, and knowledge of the resurrection must have shed new and clearer light on matters that had been obscure before. The believer can see this process as having been guided by the Holy Spirit, poured out at Pentecost. Yet nothing comes of nothing, and the origin of the astonishing character of the writings of the New Testament and the testimonies of the early Church must surely lie, where the witnesses allege it to lie, in the unique character of Jesus of Nazareth himself. The idea that he was but a shadowy figure and that all the vibrant quality of the New Testament writings originates in his followers, seems to me frankly unbelievable. I think that careful and scrupulous study of the New Testament enables one to discern the shape of a striking and original character, in whose words and deeds lie the origin of the Christian phenomenon, and who eludes classification in simply conventional religious categories, such as prophet, teacher, or healer. There has undoubtedly been development of Christological doctrine, but I do not think that there has been free invention of doctrine. This is not the place to attempt to go into a detailed defence of that judgement, but I believe that it can be done.[10]

In addition to a Christology from below, theologians can pursue also a Christology from above. Its method is not abduction from the deposits of history, but conceptual exploration of what it might mean to believe that 'the Word was made flesh' (John 1:14). Recourse to this kind of thinking grew over the centuries as the Church struggled to find the most philosophically satisfactory understanding and exposition of its core beliefs. In the process, the technical vocabulary of Greek thought was called upon, and partly transformed to make it as fit as possible for the purpose in hand. Terms such as hypostasis (individual reality) and ousia (generic substance) were pressed into theological service. In fact the distinction in meaning between these two Greek words was a fruit of these theological struggles, for they had previously been treated as synonyms. Some of this sometimes precarious discourse may have been overbold in its estimate of the extent to which finite human thought can articulate infinite mystery, but it seemed that the attempt had to be made. If theological argument from above is to find a cousinly parallel in the context of science, it lies in those creative leaps of intellectual imagination of the kind that enabled Newton to conceive of universal gravity or Einstein to write down the equations of general relativity. Even the most bold of theological speculations scarcely exceed in daring the conjectures of the string theorists.

So far this discussion has been conducted without the explicit recognition of the disturbing presence of an elephant in the room (as the saying goes). This troublesome pachyderm is the actual diversity of world religious beliefs. The context of science is effectively a universal context. There can be much argument and dissent along the way, but when the dust finally settles on a scientific issue, there is an impressive degree of unanimity that the right answer has been found. We all believe in quarks. However, in a world perspective, the context of religion is a fragmented context. I have been seeking to outline some of the motivations that lead me to embrace Christian belief, but I am well aware that my brothers and sisters in the other great world faith traditions also believe that they have good motivations for their beliefs. There are commonalities between the faiths, such as respect for the value of compassion and for the validity of unitive mystical experience, understood as encounter with sacred reality, but there are also manifest conflicts of cognitive belief. These do not only refer to core convictions, such as Christian belief in the divinity of Christ, or Islamic belief in the absolute authority of the divinely dictated Qur'an, but they also include fundamental metaphysical understandings. Is the individual human person of abiding value and significance, or something that is recycled through the turning of the samsaric wheel of reincarnation, or ultimately is it an illusion from which to seek release?

One of the most persuasive reasons for accepting scientific beliefs is the way in which, time and again, they are universally accepted as being well motivated. Does not the very variety of actual religious belief show that in reality it lacks adequate motivation? Can these beliefs really amount to anything more than simply being collections of culturally influenced opinions? One might stick for a moment with the elephant theme, recalling the parable of its inspection by blind men, one holding the trunk, another a leg, and a third the tail, and so reaching very different and superficially incompatible conclusions. May it not be that sacred reality is so profoundly beyond adequate human grasp, that no tradition can tell more than a small fraction of its reality? Some insight may be found along these lines, but I believe that the problem is much more complex than that. Interfaith perplexities are among the most difficult and challenging of those faced by religion today and I believe that they may well remain so for a long while, possibly throughout the third millennium. Genuine dialogue, and real attempts to face the issues, are only just beginning and the going will often be hard and painful.[11]

The context of science may offer some modest help as this great truth-seeking encounter between the faiths gets under way. One kind of potential assistance is simply encouragement to continue to wrestle with the problems posed and not to try to go for some quick and facile way out of perplexity, for example of the kind that a lowest common denominator view of a basic world religion might seem to offer.

So bland an account compares unfavourably with the vitality of the separate traditions and it does not do justice to the richness of religious life. Between 1900 and 1925, the physicists knew two things about light. Those who did diffraction experiments knew that it exhibited clear wave-like properties. Those who did a different set of experiments, investigating phenomena such as the photoelectric effect, knew that light exhibited equally clear particle-like properties. No one knew how to reconcile these two seemingly incompatible claims. Yet no progress would have been made by attempting to discard one or other of these sets of experience. The physicists just had to hold on as best they could, by the skin of their intellectual teeth. In the end, their patient endurance was rewarded, and modern quantum theory successfully resolved what had threated to be an intransigent paradox. Religious people may well need similar persistent fortitude as they face the apparent incompatibilities between the faiths.

The second way in which the context of science may prove helpful is by providing a meeting place for the world faiths where they can discuss together serious issues without encountering the sort of defensiveness that would inhibit dialogue.[12] If the discussion tries to start immediately with core issues, such as how one should think about Jesus, or Muhammad, or the Buddha, at once the barricades will go up and the possibility of real contact will be lost. If the discussion starts, say, with exploring how the different traditions relate modern scientific insights to the interpretion of their ancient scriptures, then it will be concerned with an important issue, but one that is not so threatening as to halt the conversation at the start. Pioneer programmes bringing together scientists from different world faiths have already shown that some progress can be made in this fashion.[13] I believe that those who come to the table in this manner must do so expressing, humbly but clearly, the understandings that they believe their tradition has given them. I do not doubt that I have many things I need to learn from my brothers and sisters in the other faiths, but when we meet it would be disingenuous for me to try to disguise my motivated belief in the unique saving significance of Jesus of Nazareth, the Son of God.

7

Eschatology

The final chapter of every story told by science, whether concerning individual beings or the universe itself, ends in death. Within the naturalistic context of science, which can only offer a 'horizontal' account corresponding to the continued unfolding of present process, no ground can be discovered for belief in anything lying beyond death. All must eventually end in seeming futility. Human beings die, on a time scale of tens of years. The universe itself will die, on a time scale of many billions of years. From the point of view of physics, this prevalence of futility is a consequence of the second law of thermodynamics, decreeing an inevitable drift from order to disorder. From the point of view of biology, evolutionary process requires the death of one generation as the price of the new life of the next.

However, science's story is not the only story to be told, and theology has a different tale to tell. Its account includes a 'vertical' dimension, corresponding to trust in the eternal faithfulness of God, and that introduces a motivated element of hope. Jesus made just this point when he was involved in an argument with the Sadducees about whether there was a destiny beyond death (Mark 12:18–27). He pointed them to the God of Abraham, Isaac, and Jacob, whom he declared to be 'not God of the dead, but of the living'. The argument is a powerful one. If the patriarchs mattered to God once, as they certainly did, then they must matter to that faithful God for ever. They were not cast aside at their deaths, as if they had served their purpose and were then just broken pots that could be discarded as being of no further use or value. In the context of theology, there is the hope of a destiny beyond death precisely because, according to its more profound understanding, the last word lies with God and not with mortality.

Since the hope thus expressed is not a natural expectation, science does not have any direct power to speak about it, either for or against. In this fundamental sense, the context of science is irrelevant to theology's task of eschatological thinking. Yet in a subsidiary sense, the context of science has a relevance to which careful attention needs to be paid. While the basis for the hope of a destiny beyond death lies in divine faithfulness – for the Christian manifested and guaranteed by the resurrection of Christ – the detailed form of discourse in which that hope is expressed may rightly be influenced by scientific understanding. The reason for this lies in the fact that a credible account of another life beyond this one has to include within it elements of both continuity and discontinuity in relation to life in this world.[1] On the one hand, it really must be Abraham, Isaac, and Jacob who live again in the Kingdom of God, and not just new characters given the old names for old time's sake. Hence the need for a criterion of continuity. On the other hand, there would be little point in making the patriarchs alive again if they were soon to die again. Hence the need for the criterion of discontinuity between this world of mortality and the world to come, of which it is said 'death shall be no more, neither shall there be mourning nor crying nor pain anymore, for the former things have passed away' (Revelation 21:4).

Science has a legitimate role to play in helping theology explore what these criteria might imply. In theological thinking there has to be an element of mystery involved in trying to speak about matters which necessarily go beyond the finite compass of present human experience. This is particularly true of eschatology, with its concern for the nature of the world to come. No doubt there comes a point in eschatological speculation at which 'wait and see' is the best advice to follow. Yet modest exploration of rational possibility, capable of being assisted by insights derived from the context of science, is worth pursuing as far as it may prove possible to do so. The exercise is similar to the way in which scientists use simplified 'thought experiments' to explore the consistency and content of new physical ideas. We turn first to the criterion of continuity.

Continuity

The carrier of the continuity of personhood between this life and the life to come has traditionally been considered to be the human soul. Often the soul has been conceived in a Platonic/Cartesian fashion as the distinct spiritual component of the person, an element that is separable from the body and released at death, which God will eventually reimbody in a great final act of resurrection. Sometimes this spiritual soul has been considered to possess its own intrinsic immortality, and sometimes its preservation post mortem has been considered to depend upon the faithful action of God.

Earlier in this book we argued for a view of persons as psychosomatic unities, not separably divisible into material and spiritual components. Does this mean then that the idea of the soul as the carrier of continuity has been irretrievably lost? I do not think so, but in the context of science the soul will need to be reconceived in non-dualist terms. What must be looked for is some way of understanding the essence of individual personhood, so that one can identify the 'real me' that is capable of continuous preservation within the flux of change. In actual fact, it is almost as challenging to know what this essential personal nature might be within this life as it is to conceive of it beyond this life. What makes me today, an elderly, bald academic, the same person as the young schoolboy with the shock of black hair in the school photograph of many years ago? At first sight it might seem tempting to suggest material continuity, but in fact this is an illusion. The actual physical atoms of our bodies are changing all the time, through wear and tear, eating and drinking. We live in a state of material flux. I am atomically distinct from that schoolboy. It is not enduring constituent stability that makes us the same person, but a more subtle kind of continuity, relating to the almost infinitely complex information-bearing pattern associated at any given time with my material body. It is this information-bearing pattern that is the way in which to think about the soul understood in the scientific context of human psychosomatic unity. Part of that pattern is the reservoir of our memories, a significant source of human belief in the possession of a continuous personality.

A number of comments need to be made. Some encouragement to this line of thinking is given by the suggestion made earlier (chapter 4) that, as science begins to study the behaviour of complex systems considered in their totalities, it seems likely that some generalised concept of information will take its place alongside energy as a category of fundamental scientific significance. Of course, if the notion of information is to be applied to human personhood in this way, it would require vast extension and elaboration beyond its comparatively banal uses in communication theory or the description of the behaviour of dissipative physical systems. It would have to possess not only a richness compatible with representing internal states characterised by value as well as by dynamical pattern, but it would also have to extend to embrace the nexus of external relationships that do so much to constitute us as persons. To be perfectly frank, currently we have no idea of how this vast generalisation might be formulated. Speaking of questions of this degree of complexity, Thomas Nagel coined a just and striking phrase when he said that our contemporary efforts to formulate dual-aspect monism as an account of the human person amount to 'nothing more than pre-Socratic flailing about'.[2] Anaximenes and Anaximander and the rest did not get very near to identifying the basic stuff out of which the variety of the world is made, but they were looking in the right direction when thinking that such a kind of stuff might exist. (One might see them as proto-elementary particle physicists, two and a half millennia too early to know about quarks!) Any contemporary attempt to speak about the nature of personhood cannot hope to prove to be much more than an analogous form of hand-waving. Nevertheless, we have to do the best we can, and I believe that 'information' is the right direction in which to wave.

Further encouragement to pursue this point of view derives from the recognition that it is a revival in modern dress of an idea with an ancient and respectable intellectual pedigree. The Aristotelian-Thomistic tradition spoke of the soul as the form of the body, and there is an obvious kinship between this idea and the information approach. The modern picture may lay greater stress on the relational aspects of personhood and be more concerned with a dynamical account, corresponding to the way in which the soul develops as character is formed and memories accumulate (the pattern grows in complexity), but the two approaches are clearly related. The notion of the soul as being an information-bearing pattern may not presently amount to much more than offering a toy of thought with which to play, but I believe that it serves to show that the acceptance of human psychosomatic unity, so natural in the context of science, does not deprive one of the idea of a carrier of continuing identity.[3]

The information-bearing pattern carried by a person's body will dissolve at death with the decay of that body. According to this picture, there is no natural immortality of the soul. Once again we recognise the extremely limited eschatological reach of science's horizontal story. Yet nothing forbids additional recourse to theology's vertical story of divine faithfulness. It is perfectly coherent to suppose that God will not allow the individual information-bearing pattern to be lost at a person's death, but will preserve it within the divine memory. Such a persisting but disembodied existence would not in itself constitute the continuation of fully personal life beyond death, because true human life is psychosomatic in its character. Its restoration would require God's further act of re-embodying that pattern in an act of resurrection in some new environment of God's choosing. If humans are psychosomatic beings, then true humanity requires some form of embodiment, though not necessarily in the flesh and blood of this world. (In fact, Paul rightly said that 'flesh and blood cannot inherit the kingdom of God, nor does the perishable inherit the imperishable'; 1 Corinthians 15:50). It is certainly consonant with the context of science that Christianity expresses its hope of a destiny beyond death in terms of death and resurrection. The notion of disembodied spiritual survival is far less persuasive to the scientific mind.

The character of the new environment (the 'new creation') must be such that it is no longer the realm of transience and death. This is the criterion of discontinuity, to whose consideration we shall shortly turn. Before doing so, we need to note two further elements of continuity, which, taking the present context of science seriously, may prove also to be features of the world to come. Human persons are not only psychosomatic beings, but they are also temporal beings. This seems to be an intrinsic aspect of humanity, and if that is so there will also need to be some form of 'time' in the world to come if true human life is to be restored at the resurrection of the dead. This 'time' may be expected to be distinct from the time of this world, being neither the latter's continuation nor its sequel, but an independent form of temporality relating to the world of God's new creation. Closely connected with time is the unfolding of process. If the history of this world teaches us anything about God it is surely that the Creator is patient and subtle, content to work though gradual development, rather than by instantaneous magic. Thus it is reasonable to anticipate that the life of the world to come will not be focused in a timeless moment of illumination, as some eschatological traditions have suggested (the beatific vision), but it will take the form of an evolving salvific process, involving judgement and purgation and leading to the endless exploration of the inexhaustible riches of the divine nature as they are progressively unveiled. If finite creatures are truly to encounter the infinite reality of the divine, it must surely be through such a 'temporal' process of this kind.[4] The finite cannot take in the Infinite at a single glance.

Discontinuity

We have seen that mortality is endemic in this world for two fundamental reasons. One is that the fertility of evolutionary biological process depends upon there being a succession of the generations, so that death is a necessary feature of this stage of creation. New life has to be able to appear and take over from that which had preceded it, as creatures make themselves. The second and related reason, which explains physically how universal transience and decay actually occur, lies in the operation of the second law of thermodynamics, whose consequence is that isolated complex systems inevitably drift from order to disorder. Even dissipative systems cannot avoid this drift for ever, for the increase of entropy (disorder) is statistically driven. Since there are overwhelmingly more ways of being disorderly than there are of being orderly, in the end the rising waters of chaos are bound to engulf the little islands of order.

However, it does not seem incoherent to believe that God could bring into being a new kind of 'matter', endowed with such strong self-organising principles that it would not be condemned to a thermodynamic descent into chaos. Theology can envisage this new form of 'matter' as arising from the divine transformation of present matter, redeeming it from its otherwise inevitable end in cosmic futility. On this view, the eschatological destinies of human beings and of the whole universe lie together in the world of God's new creation (cf. Romans 8:19–21). This new creation is not a second divine attempt at creatio ex nihilo, an action which would seem to imply the ultimate irrelevance of the first creation, but rather it is a creatio ex vetere, the transformation of the old into the new. In Christian thinking, the seed event from which this new creation has already begun to grow is the resurrection of Christ. His tomb was empty because the matter of his corpse had been transmuted into the 'matter' of the new creation, to become his risen and glorified body in which he appeared to the first witnesses. In Christ there is a destiny for matter as well as for people (cf. Colossians 1:15–20).[5]

A final question remains to be addressed. If the new creation, free from death and suffering, is to be so wonderful, why was it not brought into being straight away? Why did God bother with the old creation, this world of transience and decay? I believe that the answer lies in recognising that kenotic creation is intrinsically a two-stage act. First must come a world in which creatures exist at a sufficient distance from the infinite reality of their Creator so that they are allowed a true freedom to be themselves. If finite creatures are not to be overwhelmed, the divine presence must initially be veiled. The process of that world will be an evolutionary process in which creatures are allowed to make themselves, as potentiality is explored and brought to birth. We have seen that mortality is intrinsic to such an evolving world, which has to be poised at the edge of chaos. The old creation will fulfil some of the divine creative purposes, but not all of them. God's final intention is to draw all who will freely come, into closer contact with the divine life, so that they may live in the light of progressively unveiled divine reality to the utmost extent to which it is possible for finite beings to share in that infinite reality. True fullness of life will come through this everlasting encounter, and there will be no need for the evolutionary sequence of finite generations. Theologically we may say that the world of the new creation will be the realm where final eschatological fulfilment will be attained through a panentheistic participation in divine reality (1 Corinthians 15:28).[6] In Christian understanding, this ultimate sacramental participation by creatures in the divine life is made possible by the bridge established by the incarnate Son of God between the life of God and the life of creation.

This deep and hopeful mystery takes us into a realm of truth lying far beyond the context of science, and it makes fully intelligible what is the ultimate point of the fruitful, but seemingly imperfect, world that science is privileged to explore. Reflecting on the eventual futility of this present world, the distinguished theoretical physicist and staunch atheist Steven Weinberg notoriously commented that the more the universe seemed comprehensible to him, the more it also seemed to be pointless.[7] With only the horizontal story of an unrelenting naturalism to tell, one can understand how he reached this verdict. Theology, however, asserts that there is more to be said. What a credible eschatology is seeking to establish is that the divine creation is truly and everlastingly a cosmos and not, as Weinberg feared, ultimately a chaos whose final end must lie in futility. The message of eschatological hope is that the world makes sense, now and always.

Postscript
Understanding

—•◆•—

Research in science is hard work. Like any other worthwhile activity, it has its fair share of wearisome routine. It also has its fair share of frustration and disappointed hopes, as the good ideas of the morning prove less persuasive in the cold light of the afternoon. So why do scientists do it? Certainly not merely to be able to invent new devices and discover novel ways of accomplishing practical purposes. Valuable though these consequences of scientific advance can be, they are properly the concern of science's lusty offspring technology, rather than of pure science itself. Pure science derives its prime motivation from the desire to understand. Science is a part of the great human quest to achieve a degree of comprehension of the nature of reality that is as fully adequate as possible to the actual richness of that reality. It focuses on gaining knowledge of what the world is made of, how it works, and what its history has been. Science has been spectacularly successful in this endeavour. However, we have seen that the thirst for understanding through and through will never be quenched by science alone. Science's self-defining restriction to considering only certain kinds of impersonal experience, and to asking only certain limited sorts of question, leaves too much uninvestigated and unaddressed for that to be possible. We have noted the metaquestions of cosmic intelligibility and wonderful order, and of cosmic fine-tuning, that arise from scientific insights, but whose answering necessarily lies outside the confines of science itself. The reality of personhood, with its rich spectrum of different kinds of encounter with reality, must also be taken with the utmost seriousness. Science's technique of bracketing out the personal may be methodologically effective, but metaphysically it is disastrously impoverished.

Hence the need for a more extensive and profound context of understanding, an enlargement of the rational pursuit of truth –

attainable through an extended search for motivated belief – which can profit from drawing upon theological insight. Yet if theology is indeed to make its proper contribution, it must in its turn be sensitive to the contextual influence of its scientific partner, both in relation to those matters of specialised understanding which science uniquely can offer in its own domain, and also in relation to styles of thought that can fruitfully play a part in shaping the character of the interaction between science and religion.

The search for understanding within science itself is often characterised by a progression from initial rather rough and ready modelling of what is going on in some new class of phenomena, to the eventual discovery of an overarching theory that is comprehensive in the understanding that flows from it and which is deep in its conceptual subtlety. In fundamental physics, the theories thus eventually attained have consistently turned out to be rationally beautiful and intellectually rewarding, for they are based on controlling principles which, though they may be counterintuitive in terms of previous thinking, are persuasively illuminating and mentally satisfying. The history of quantum physics exemplifies the point.

In 1900 Max Planck daringly suggested that radiation from a heated body might be emitted in discrete packets of energy (quanta). Instead of the radiation oozing out like water from a spring, Planck conceived it as being like the succession of separate drops of water dripping from a tap. Thirteen years later, Niels Bohr gave an insightful account of the hydrogen atom, formulated by extending the idea that physical quantities come in countable packets. Both these pioneering moves resulted in predictions that were empirically successful, but both were results of an inspired tinkering with classical physics of an apparently ad hoc kind, whose consistency was open to considerable doubt. To be convincing and intellectually satisfying, what was needed was an overarching theory, clearly and consistently formulated. That theory came with astonishing rapidity in the anni mirabiles of 1925–26, when Werner Heisenberg and Erwin Schrödinger each produced their versions of a complete quantum mechanics. Almost immediately, Paul Dirac identified the superposition principle as the foundational concept that distinguished quantum physics from its classical Newtonian predecessor. Modern quantum theory is much more sophisticated, and its mathematical formulation looks much more complicated, than the models of Planck and Bohr that preceded it, but the earlier models were essential staging-posts on the way to a comprehensive understanding.

Christian theology also exemplifies an analogous progression. The writers of the New Testament drew on their Jewish tradition in the attempt to find ways of expressing their experience of Jesus and his resurrection. In this quest they appropriated various titles from the Hebrew scriptures, such as Messiah (Christ), Lord, Son of God, which they used as models to apply to this known figure of recent history. Yet the intermingling of human and divine-sounding language in their discourse about the risen Jesus left many issues unresolved. (One might even describe those early Christian ideas as having been the result of inspired tinkerings with the Jewish prophetic tradition.) Several centuries of subsequent theological struggle and argument eventually led the Church to the doctrine of the incarnation, the understanding of Jesus of Nazareth as the Word of God made flesh, classically expressed in 451 at the Council of Chalcedon. Because theology is intrinsically more difficult than science, its theory-making has been less comprehensively successful. Yet there is a clear analogy between the search for Christological understanding in theology and the search for quantum understanding in physics.[1]

We have been considering the practice of theology in the context of science. The metacontext which contains both scientific and theological discourse is the great human quest for truth and understanding, pursued with the utmost seriousness and without reserve. In the tradition of theological thinking that stems from Thomas Aquinas, such an unrestricted search for understanding is recognised as being ultimately the search for God, whether those engaged upon it know that or not. Bernard Lonergan wrote of God as 'the unrestricted act of understanding, the eternal rapture glimpsed in every Archimedean cry of Eureka'.[2]

Notes

Introduction

1 J. C. Polkinghorne, *Science and Christian Belief/The Faith of a Physicist*, SPCK, 1994/Fortress, 1996.
2 J. C. Polkinghorne, *Science and the Trinity*, SPCK/Yale University Press, 2004.
3 See, J. C. Polkinghorne, *Quantum Physics and Theology*, SPCK/Yale University Press, 2007.
4 See, J. C. Polkinghorne, *Quantum Theory: A Very Short Introduction*, Oxford University Press, 2002, pp. 37–38, 87.
5 M. Polanyi, *Personal Knowledge*, Routledge and Kegan Paul, 1958.

1 Contextual theology

1 See, J. C. Polkinghorne, *Science and the Trinity*, SPCK/Yale University Press, 2004, ch. 2.
2 I. G. Barbour, *Issues in Science and Religion*, SCM Press, 1966; and subsequent writings.
3 Quoted in J. H. Brooke, *Science and Religion*, Cambridge University Press, 1991, p. 314.
4 R. Williams, *On Christian Theology*, Blackwell, 2000, p. xiv.
5 For an example, see D. F. Ford and R. Muers (eds), *The Modern Theologians* (3rd edition), Blackwell, 2005.
6 W. Pannenberg, *Anthropology in a Theological Perspective*, Westminster, 1985.
7 W. Pannenberg, *Towards a Theology of Nature*, Westminster/John Knox, 1993, p. 16.
8 See, J. C. Polkinghorne, *Faith, Science and Understanding*, SPCK/Yale University Press, 2000, pp. 156–173.
9 See especially, Pannenberg, *Theology of Nature*.
10 W. Pannenberg in C. R. Albright and J. Haugen (eds), *Beginning with the End*, Open Court, 1997, p. 251.
11 J. C. Polkinghorne, *Exploring Reality*, SPCK/Yale University Press, 2005, ch. 2.
12 Pannenberg, *Anthropology*, p. 520.
13 J. C. Polkinghorne, *The God of Hope and the End of the World*, SPCK/Yale University Press, 2002.
14 Polkinghorne, *Faith, Science and Understanding*, ch. 7.

15 A. R. Peacocke, *Creation and the World of Science*, Oxford University Press, 1979, pp. 105–107.
16 See, Polkinghorne, *Faith, Science and Understanding*, pp. 173–185.
17 B. Lonergan, *Insight*, Longman, 1958.
18 E. L. Mascall, *Christian Theology and Natural Science*, Longman, 1956.

2 Discourse

1 For an account of the ideas of quantum theory, see J. C. Polkinghorne, *Quantum Theory: A Very Short Introduction*, Oxford University Press, 2002.
2 Ibid., pp. 37–38.
3 T. F. Torrance, *Theological Science*, Oxford University Press, 1969, p. 9.
4 See, J. C. Polkinghorne, *Beyond Science*, Cambridge University Press, 1996, ch. 2; *Quantum Theory*, ch. 6.
5 B. Lonergan, *Insight*, Longman, 1958, pp. 684, 645.
6 See, for example, I. G. Barbour, *Issues in Science and Religion*, SCM Press, 1966, chs 6–9; *Science and Religion*, SCM Press, 1998, chs 4–6; A. R. Peacocke, *Intimations of Reality*, University of Notre Dame Press, 1984; *Theology for a Scientific Age*, SCM Press, 1993, pp. 11–23; J. C. Polkinghorne, *Reason and Reality*, SPCK/Trinity Press International, 1991, chs 1–2; *Belief in God in an Age of Science*, Yale University Press, 1998, chs 3 and 5; *Quantum Physics and Theology*, SPCK/Yale University Press, 2007.
7 J. C. Polkinghorne, *Science and Christian Belief/The Faith of a Physicist*, SPCK, 1994/Fortress, 1996.
8 J. C. Polkinghorne, *Faith, Science and Understanding*, SPCK/Yale University Press, 2000, ch. 1.
9 Polkinghorne, *Science and Christian Belief/Faith of a Physicist*; in both editions the subtitle is 'Theological Reflections of a Bottom-up Thinker'.
10 J. C. Polkinghorne, *Science and Providence* (2nd edition), Templeton Foundation Press, 2005, ch. 4.
11 Polkinghorne, *Quantum Physics and Theology*.
12 See, Polkinghorne, *Beyond Science*, ch. 2.
13 Ibid., and J. C. Polkinghorne, *Rochester Roundabout*, Longman/W. H. Freeman, 1989, ch. 21.
14 M. Polanyi, *Personal Knowledge*, Routledge and Kegan Paul, 1958.
15 Here I differ somewhat from the stance taken by my scientist-theologian colleague Arthur Peacocke; see the discussion in J. C. Polkinghorne, *Science and the Trinity*, SPCK/Yale University Press, 2004, ch. 1.
16 For concise surveys see, for example, I. G. Barbour, *Ethics in an Age of Technology*, HarperCollins, 1993; C. Deane-Drummond, *Biology and Theology Today*, SCM Press, 2001.

17 For my views on specific ethical issues related to genetic advances, see J. C. Polkinghorne, *Exploring Reality*, SPCK/Yale University Press, 2005, ch. 9.

18 Ibid., pp. 153–156.

19 Lynn White, *Science 155*, 1967, pp. 1203–1207.

3 Time and space

1 S. Weinberg, *The First Three Minutes*, Andre Deutsch, 1977.

2 C. de Duve, *Vital Dust*, Basic Books, 1995.

3 J. Monod, *Chance and Necessity*, Collins, 1972; F. Crick, *Life Itself*, McDonald, 1982.

4 One might say the same about the possibility of there being other created universes, different and distinct from this one, a possibility which the currently discussed notion of a multiverse raises in a highly speculative fashion.

5 A form of simultaneous influence is possible in systems of quantum entanglement, but this is because intrinsically they are not separable in the normal way. The strict statement of special relativity is that messages to synchronise clocks (information) cannot be propagated faster than light, and quantum entanglement cannot be used for this purpose. For a sophisticated discussion of the issues raised, see B. d'Espagnat, *On Physics and Philosophy*, Princeton University Press, 2006.

6 For a debate on the issue, see C. J. Isham and J. C. Polkinghorne, in R. J. Russell, N. Murphy, and C. J. Isham (eds), *Quantum Cosmology and the Laws of Nature*, Vatican Observatory/CTNS, 1993, pp. 135–144.

7 Cosmic time is defined by the frame of reference at rest with respect to the cosmic background radiation.

8 See, J. C. Polkinghorne, *Faith, Science and Understanding*, SPCK/Yale University Press, 2000, ch. 7.

9 See, for example, C. Pinnock et al., *The Openness of God*, IVP, 1994.

10 J. C. Polkinghorne, *Science and Creation* (2nd edition), Templeton Foundation Press, 2006, pp. 81–83.

11 A. N. Whitehead, *Process and Reality* (corrected edition), Free Press, 1978; see also, C. Hartshorne, *Divine Reality*, Yale University Press, 1948.

12 See the essays in J. C. Polkinghorne (ed.), *The Work of Love*, Eerdmans/SPCK, 2001.

13 Ibid., pp. 102–105. I suggest also a kenosis of causal status, as God condescends to act providentially as a cause among causes, acting interactively within the open grain of nature in an unfolding universe.

14 I. G. Barbour, *Religion in an Age of Science*, SCM Press, 1990; A. R. Peacocke, *Theology in a Scientific Age*, SCM Press, 1993; J. C. Polkinghorne, *Science and Christian Belief/The Faith of a Physicist*, SPCK, 1994/Fortress, 1996.

4 Persons and value

1 For a detailed analysis of the inadequacy of naturalism, see J. Haught, *Is Nature Enough?*, Cambridge University Press, 2006.
2 See, for example, J. W. van Huyssteen, *Duet or Duel?*, SCM Press, 1998; F. M. Wuketits, *Evolutionary Epistemology*, SUNY Press, 1990.
3 M. Polanyi, *Personal Knowledge*, Routledge and Kegan Paul, 1958.
4 J. C. Polkinghorne, *Exploring Reality*, SPCK/Yale University Press, 2005, pp. 35–36, 57–58.
5 S. Kauffman, *At Home in the Universe*, Oxford University Press, 1995, ch. 4.
6 I. Prigogine and I. Stengers, *Order out of Chaos*, Heinemann, 1984.
7 See, H. C. von Baeyer, *Information*, Weidenfeld and Nicolson, 2003.
8 D. Bohm and B. Hiley, *The Undivided Universe*, Routledge, 1993.
9 J. C. Polkinghorne, *Belief in God in an Age of Science*, Yale University Press, 1998, ch. 3.
10 I. Prigogine, *The End of Certainty*, Free Press, 1996.
11 Polkinghorne, *Exploring Reality*, ch. 2.
12 Polkinghorne, *Belief in God*, ch. 3.
13 J. Searle, *Minds, Brains and Science*, BBC Publications, 1984 (see especially his celebrated 'Chinese Room' parable, pp. 32–36); R. Penrose, *The Emperor's New Mind*, Oxford University Press, 1989, ch. 9.
14 Polkinghorne, *Exploring Reality*, ch. 3.
15 See, Polkinghorne, *Belief in God*, ch. 6.
16 D. J. Chalmers, *The Conscious Mind*, Oxford University Press, 1996.
17 As claimed in D. C. Dennett, *Consciousness Explained*, Little, Brown, 1991.
18 For example, Polkinghorne, *Belief in God*, ch. 1; *Science and Creation* (2nd edition), Templeton Foundation Press, 2006, chs 1 and 2.
19 P. W. Davies, *The Mind of God*, Simon and Schuster, 1992.

5 Consonance: creation, providence, and relationality

1 S. W. Hawking, *A Brief History of Time*, Bantam, 1988, p. 141.
2 Ibid., p. 174.
3 J. D. Barrow and F. J. Tipler, *The Anthropic Cosmological Principle*, Oxford University Press, 1986; J. Leslie, *Universes*, Routledge, 1989; R. D. Holder, *God, the Multiverse and Everything*, Ashgate, 2004. The insight would better have been called 'the carbon principle', since its concern is with the generality of carbon-based lfe, rather than the specificity of homo sapiens.
4 In quantum physics, empty space (the vacuum) is not permitted by Heisenberg's uncertainty principle to be totally quiescent. Instead it is a seething sea of 'vacuum fluctuations'. These generate an energy associated with space itself that would be immense but for the fact that

remarkable cancellations have apparently reduced its magnitude by a factor of 10^{-120} to give the anthropically acceptable value that we actually observe.

5 This parable is borrowed from John Leslie.

6 The argument is not as straightforward as it might seem at first sight. To take a simple example, there is an infinite number of even integers, but you will never find one with the property of oddness among them.

7 B. Greene, *The Elegant Universe*, Jonathan Cape, 1999; L. Susskind, *The Cosmic Landscape*, Little, Brown, 2006; for critiques, see L. Smolin, *The Trouble with Physics*, Allen Lane, 2006; P. Woit, *Not Even Wrong*, Jonathan Cape, 2006.

8 Change of scale by sixteen orders of magnitude would take one from a city the size of Cambridge to much less than a single atom.

9 J. Monod, *Chance and Necessity*, Collins, 1972.

10 A. R. Peacocke, *Creation and the World of Science*, Oxford University Press, 1979; *God and the New Biology*, Dent, 1986; *Theology for a Scientific Age*, SCM Press, 1993.

11 See, P. Clayton, *Mind and Emergence*, Oxford University Press, 2004.

12 J. C. Polkinghorne, *Science and Providence* (2nd edition), Templeton Foundation Press, 2005, pp. 77–78.

13 See, R. J. Russell, N. Murphy, and A. R. Peacocke (eds), *Chaos and Complexity*, CTNS/Vatican Observatory, 1995; R. J. Russell, P. Clayton, K. Wegter-McNelly, and J. C. Polkinghorne (eds), *Quantum Mechanics*, CTNS/Vatican Observatory, 2001; J. C. Polkinghorne, *Belief in God in an Age of Science*, Yale University Press, 1998, ch. 3.

14 J. C. Polkinghorne, *Exploring Reality*, SPCK/Yale University Press, 2005, ch. 2.

15 See, J. C. Polkinghorne, *Quantum Theory: A Very Short Introduction*, Oxford University Press, 2002, ch. 5.

16 Here is another example of how epistemology must conform to actual ontology. The quantum world can be known only in accord with its non-local nature. Approaches based on the expectation of a strictly separable objectivity are condemned to fail.

17 See, Polkinghorne, *Exploring Reality*, ch. 2, for a fuller discussion.

18 J. Zizioulas, *Being as Communion*, St Vladimir's Seminary Press, 1985.

19 See, J. C. Polkinghorne, *Science and the Trinity*, SPCK/Yale University Press, 2004 especially ch. 3.

6 Motivated belief

1 J. C. Polkinghorne, *Science and Christian Belief/The Faith of a Physicist*, SPCK/Fortress, 1994/1996. In both editions, the subtitle is 'Theological Reflections of a Bottom-up Thinker'.

2 See, for example, R. Dawkins, *The God Delusion*, Bantam Press, 2006.

3 See, for example, J. C. Polkinghorne, *Belief in God in an Age of Science*, Yale University Press, 1998, ch. 1; A. Monti, *A Natural Theology of the Arts*, Ashgate, 2003.

4 See, M. Jammer, *Einstein and Religion*, Princeton University Press, 1999.

5 See, J. C. Polkinghorne, *Science and the Trinity*, SPCK/Yale University Press, 2004, ch. 2.

6 Polkinghorne, *Science and Christian Belief/Faith of a Physicist*, especially chs 5–7; J. C. Polkinghorne and M. Welker, *Faith in the Living God*, SPCK/Fortress, 2001.

7 See, J. C. Polkinghorne, *The God of Hope and the End of the World*, SPCK/Yale University Press, 2002, pp. 120–122.

8 N. T. Wright, *The Resurrection of the Son of God*, SPCK, 2003.

9 J. Moltmann, *The Crucified God*, SCM Press, 1974.

10 See especially, C. F. D. Moule, *The Origins of Christology*, Cambridge University Press, 1977; J. D. G. Dunn, *A New Perspective on Jesus*, SPCK, 2005; L. Hurtado, *Lord Jesus Christ*, Eerdmans, 2003.

11 See, Polkinghorne, *Science and Christian Belief/Faith of Physicist*, ch. 10.

12 Polkinghorne, *Belief in God*, pp. 90–92.

13 W. M. Richardson, R. J. Russell, P. Clayton, and K. Wegter-McNelly (eds), *Science and the Spiritual Quest*, Routledge, 2002.

7 Eschatology

1 J. C. Polkinghorne and M. Welker (eds), *The End of the World and the Ends of God*, Trinity Press International, 2000; J. C. Polkinghorne, *The God of Hope and the End of the World*, SPCK/Yale University Press, 2002.

2 T. Nagel, *The View from Nowhere*, Oxford University Press, 1986, p. 30.

3 Polkinghorne, *God of Hope*, ch. 9.

4 Ibid., ch. 11.

5 Ibid., ch. 10.

6 Panentheism, which asserts that the world is in God though God exceeds the world, is to be distinguished from pantheism, which equates the world and God. I do not accept panentheism as an account of the present relationship between Creator and creation, but I do believe it to be the eschatological destiny of the new creation.

7 S. Weinberg, *The First Three Minutes*, Andre Deutsch, 1977, p. 149.

Postscript: Understanding

1 For a much fuller discussion, see J. C. Polkinghorne, *Quantum Physics and Theology*, SPCK/Yale University Press, 2007.

2 B. Lonergan, *Insight*, Longman, 1958, p. 684.

Index

agency 53–4, 57
anthropic principle xx, 69–73
Aquinas, Thomas 3, 8, 41, 43
arrow of time 44–5
atheism 25, 87
Augustine, St 3–4, 33, 41

Bacon, F. 31
Barth, K. 7
becoming 40–1, 43–4
Bénard convection 52
block universe 39–1, 43–4
Boethius 41
Bohm, D. 55
bottom-up thinking xii, xv–vi, xxi,
  19–20, 86

causality xx, 37–8, 43, 53–7, 77–9
chaos theory 55–6, 78–9
Christology 89–99, 112
classical theology 41, 81
complexity theory xix, 51–3
consciousness xviii–xix, 59–60
consonance 66–8
contextual theology xi–xv, 1–8,
  17–22, 27, 66–7
contingency 10–11
continuity, criterion of 103–7
creation xvi, xix–xx, 68–77
critical realism 17, 54–5

Darwin, C. 4, 61
death of Christ 26, 97–8
Descartes, R. 31
dipolarity, divine xviii, 41–3
Dirac, P. A. M. 15, 60–1, 111
discontinuity, criterion of 107–8
dissipative systems 44, 82
dual-aspect monism 50, 105

Einstein, A. 12, 25, 38–9, 49, 81–2
Epicurus 76
epistemology 15
eschatology xxi–xxii, 102–9
ethics xvi–xvii, 27–32, 63–4, 73–6
evolution xvi, xix–xx, 47–8, 58–9,
  64, 107
experiment 22
extraterrestrial life 35–6

Faraday, M. 13
field 9–10, 13
futility xxi, 34, 83, 102
future, priority of 11

Galileo 2, 4, 25, 36
God and time xvii, 41–2
Gödel, K. 3, 24

Haldane, J. B. S. 13–14
Hawking, S. W. 68
Heisenberg, W. 111
hope xxi, 102
Hume, D. 96

inertia 9
information xix, xxii, 51–3, 57–8,
  104–5
intelligibility xv, xviii–xx, 8–9,
  16–17, 48–9, 61–2, 69

Kant, I. 54
Kauffman, S. 51, 78
kenosis xvii–xviii, xx, 42–3
Kingsley, C. 75

La Mettrie, J. O. de 77
Laplace, P. S. 43–4
Lonergan, B. 12, 17, 112

Mandelbrot, B. 58
Mascall, E. 12
mathematics 48, 58–9
Maxwell, J. C. 15, 81–2
metaphysics xvii, 37, 40–1, 60,
    62
miracle 21, 93–4
Molina, L. de 43
Monod, J. 74
Moore, A. 4
motivated belief xxi, 20, 84–101
multiverse 71–3
music 63

Nagel, T. 105
natural theology xix, 61–2, 66,
    86–7
new creation 106–8
Newton, I. 13, 25, 38

open theology 41–2
Origen 26, 80

Paley, W. 61
Pannenberg, W. 8–11
paradox 18–19
Pascal, B. 46
Peacocke, A. R. 11, 75
persons xviii, 22–4, 34–5, 46–65
Planck, M. 16, 19, 111
Polanyi, M. xviii, 23–5, 49, 86
prayer 80
process theology 4, 42
proof 86
providence xix–xx, 11, 77–81
psychosomatic unity 50–1, 53,
    106

quantum entanglement 81–2
quantum logic xvi, 15

quantum theory xv–xvi, 14–17, 48,
    55–6, 78–9, 111

rationality xvi, 20, 24, 84–5
Ray, J. 61
reality 16
relationality xix–xxi, 81–3
relativity 14, 37–40
resurrection xxi, 90–7
revelation xvi, 22, 87–9

Schrödinger, E. 111
science and theology compared
    xv–xvi, 17–19, 21, 23–7, 85–6
scientism xiii, 46–7
scripture 1–3, 21, 43
separability 56, 82
soul xxii, 53, 104
space 35, 37
string theory 72–3
superposition principle 14–15, 48

theodicy 76–7
thermodynamics, second law of
    44–5, 107
time xvii, 33–4, 37–45, 106
top-down causality 78
Torrance, T. F. 11–12, 15

uncertainty principle 14–15, 55
understanding 110–12

value 60–5

wave/particle duality 15–16, 18
Weinberg, S. 108
Whitehead, A. N. 4, 42
Williams, R. 5
world faiths xii, xxi, 45, 99–101
Wright, N. T. 97